by

Johna Blinn

Edited by
Tom Dorsey

PUBLISHED BY PLAYMORE INC., PUBLISHERS AND WALDMAN PUBLISHING CORP.
New York, New York
Printed in Canada/Cover Printed in the United States of America

Fabulous Cookbook Series
Prepared Under the Editorial Direction of
Joshua Hanft

Illustrated by Arthur Friedman

Designed by Irva Mandelbaum

*Cover photo: Mediterranean Chuck Stew; Smothered Chuck Stew
& Old Fashioned Oven Chuck Roast
Courtesy of Lea & Perrins Worchestershire Sauce*

To Tommy

Acknowledgments:

This writer is especially indebted to the expert advice, encouragement and cooperation of many. I am particularly indebted to Ruth Lundgren, Olive Dempsey, Chris Pines, Caryl Saunders, Claire Boasi, Anita Fial, Pat Mason, A.C. Collins, Marilyn Kaytor, Ed Justin, The Fresh Garlic Association, Lea & Perrins Worcestershire Sauce, American Mushroom Association, Tuna Research Foundation, McIlhenny Co., Anita Mizner, Howard Helmer, Prince Foods Light Pasta, Barbara Robinson, Sunkist Growers, Inc., California Milk Advisory Board, American Egg Board, Florida Celery Committee, California Iceberg Lettuce Commission, American Dairy Association, American Spice Trade Association, Virginia Schroeder, Alice Gautsch, Eileen Edwards Denne, Borden's Lite-Line Pasteurized Process Cheese Product, Quaker Oats Co., Carolyn Coughlin, California Fresh Market Tomato Advisory Board, Margaret Spader, Fleischmann's (unsalted margarine and 100% corn oil margarine), Florida Citrus Commission, National Broiler Council, Idaho Potato Commission, California Table Grape Commission, Campbell Soup Co., Angostura International Limited, Rice Council, Rae Hartfield, Betsy Slinkard, Argo and Kingsford's Corn Starch, United Fresh Fruit and Vegetable Association, Gloria Marshall, Marilyn Dompe, National Fisheries Institute, Inc., Patricia O'Keefe, California Artichoke Advisory Board, Mazola Corn Oil, Castle & Cooke Foods (Dole/Bumble Bee), Virginia Pinegreen, Donna Higgins, Del Monte Kitchens, Dot Tringali, Kay Murphy O'Flynn, Washington State Apple Commission, Dee Munson, Lois Westlund, Egg Beaters Cholesterol-free Egg Substitute, California Avocado Commission, Charcoal Briquet Institute, Alaska Seafood Marketing Institute, Washington State Potato Commission, Hellmann's and Best Foods Mayonnaise, Roxie Howlett, Diamond Walnut Kitchen, Skippy Peanut Butter, Karo Corn Syrup, Planter's Peanut Oil Test Kitchen, Standard Brands, Inc., National Turkey Federation, Christine Dozel, Jan Kerman, South African Rock Lobster Service Corporation, Nucoa Margarine, Diane Cline, Frances Fleming, Virginia Schroeder, Lawry's Ltd., California Milk Advisory Board, Ray Clark, National Duckling Council, California Bartlett Growers, Inc., O'Neal F. Caliendo, Yvonne Martin, National Capon Council, National Goose Council, National Livestock and Meat Board, American Lamb Council, Olive Administrative Committee, Fleischmann's Active Dry Yeast, Blue Bonnet Margarine, California Dried Fig Advisory Board, Beef Industry Council, Peanut Advisory Board, National Pork Producers Council, Kikkoman International Inc., New Zealand Lamb Co., Jan Works, Schiling Division McCormick and Co., National Cherry Growers & Industries Foundation, Susan Martinson, Jan Sirochman, Golden Grain Macaroni Co., Sweet Potato Council of California, Donna Hamilton, B.J. McCabe, Leafy Greens Council, Marcia L. Watts, California Turkey Industry Board, Frani Lauda, Italian Wine Center, National Macaroni Institute, J. Marsiglia, California Almond Growers Exchange, Bertolli's (olive oil, red-Italian wine vinegar, spaghetti sauce and wines), North American Blueberry Council, Fenella Pearson, Florio (dry and sweet Marsala wines), Ken Bray, 21 Brands (Liquore Galliano), Sherrie Newman, Wyler's Beef-Flavored Instant Bouillon, Jamaica Resort Hotels, Borden Company, Los Angeles Smoking and Curing Company, Mrs. Cubbison's Foods, Inc., Catherine Stratemeyer, Southern Belle English Walnuts, Denmark Cheese Association, Shirley Mack, Beans of the West, International Multifoods (Kretschmer Wheat Germ) and Imported Winter Grapes Association.

J.B.

**BARONET
B·O·O·K·S**

BARONET BOOKS is a trademark of Playmore Inc., Publishers
and Waldman Publishing Corp., New York, N.Y.

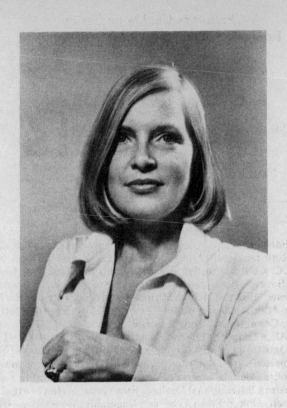

The Author

To many of the top movie and television stars, Johna Blinn is a celebrity. For almost 20 years they have welcomed her into their homes, onto sets, just about anywhere to talk about food, entertaining and lifestyles. Her column, "Celebrity Cookbook," is syndicated throughout the world and appears weekly in more than 140 newspapers and periodicals. A collection of hundreds of these conversations and recipes appears in *Celebrity Cookbook* published by Waldman Publishing Corporation.

Blinn is a former assistant food editor of LOOK magazine and is the author of a number of books, including *The Shangri-la Cookbook*. While she is busy working on her first novel and screenplay, Blinn still manages to serve as a frequent contributor of indepth interviews, profiles and entertainment features to newspapers and magazines in the U. S. and abroad.

A graduate of the State University of Iowa, Blinn took graduate work in home economics at the University of Wisconsin and taught home economics in Iowa, Virginia and New York. Now based in Los Angeles, she is married to a nationally known newspaper syndicate editor, writer and management consultant, and they have two teenage children.

CONTENTS

Marinated Beef Kabobs

Serves 6

¼ cup salad oil
2 tablespoons cider vinegar
1 teaspoon celery salt
1 teaspoon onion salt
¾ teaspoon garlic salt
¾ teaspoon oregano leaves

½ teaspoon salt
½ teaspoon ground black pepper
2 pounds boneless shoulder or
 top round of beef
6 medium-size mushroom caps
2 zucchini, cut into ½-inch pieces

1. Combine oil, vinegar, celery, onion and garlic salts, oregano, salt and black pepper in small saucepan; bring to a boil. Cool.
2. Cut meat into 1½-inch cubes; place in snug-fitting bowl with mushrooms and zucchini.
3. Add marinade; mix lightly.
4. Cover or seal; refrigerate 4 to 6 hours, turning occasionally.
5. Alternate meat and vegetables on skewers; broil on rack over hot coals or under a preheated hot broiler 10 to 15 minutes, turning and basting frequently.

Grilled Budget Chuck Steak

Serves 6

¼ cup vinegar
2 tablespoons Worcestershire
 sauce
2 tablespoons corn oil
1½ teaspoons unseasoned meat
 tenderizer

⅛ to ¼ teaspoon marjoram,
 (optional)
⅛ to ¼ teaspoon rosemary,
 (optional)
⅛ to ¼ teaspoon thyme,
 (optional)

3 pounds chuck steak, cut 1½ inches thick

1. One hour before serving, combine vinegar, Worcestershire, oil, meat tenderizer and herbs.
2. Pierce steak on all sides with pronged fork; pour vinegar mixture over steak and refrigerate 1 hour, turning once or twice.
3. Grill or broil 8 to 12 minutes on each side, basting with vinegar mixture occasionally.
4. To serve, carve into thin slices.

NOTE: Flank steak may be used in place of chuck steak. Score flank steak to keep it flat while cooking. Grill close to heat 5 minutes per side. Carve in thin slices, cutting diagonally across grain.

Szechuan Shredded Beef

Serves 6

1 pound flank steak
2 tablespoons soy sauce
1 tablespoon sherry
1 tablespoon honey
1 teaspoon cornstarch
2 cloves garlic, minced
¼ teaspoon ground ginger

1 package (6 ounces) frozen
   snow peas, thawed
2 medium carrots
3 green onions
4 tablespoons corn oil
½ teaspoon salt
¼ teaspoon crushed red pepper

1. Roll up flank steak, jellyroll fashion, lengthwise along grain of meat.
2. Cut ⅛ to ¼-inch thick slices, across grain, forming long, thin shreds.
3. Mix together soy sauce, sherry, honey, cornstarch, garlic and ginger in medium-size bowl.
4. Add meat and toss to coat evenly; set aside.
5. Cut snow peas in half lengthwise; cut carrots and green onions into 1½-inch-long matchstick-style shreds.
6. Heat 2 tablespoons corn oil in large skillet or wok over medium-high heat; add snow peas, carrots and green onions; cook, stirring quickly, 3 minutes, or until tender-crisp.
7. Add salt. Remove vegetables from skillet.
8. Heat remaining oil over medium-high heat; add meat and cook, stirring quickly, 3 minutes, or until meat loses its pink color.
9. Add red pepper; return vegetables to skillet and toss together.

Minute Steak Bordelaise

Serves 4

2 tablespoons butter
1 medium onion, sliced
1 clove garlic (optional)
1 cup beef broth or bouillon
1 tablespoon cornstarch, dissolved in
   2 tablespoons water

⅔ cup dry red wine
2 tablespoons sherry
salt to taste
pepper to taste
1 pound minute (sandwich) steaks
parsley (optional garnish)

1. Melt butter in skillet; cook onion and garlic until limp.
2. Stir in beef broth and dissolved cornstarch; heat to boiling, stirring until sauce thickens.
3. Stir in red wine and sherry; season with salt and pepper.
4. Pour sauce into saucepan and keep warm.
5. Add minute steaks to original skillet; raise heat and cook, turning occasionally until evenly browned, about 90 seconds.
6. Remove steaks to serving platter; pour sauce over them and serve family style.
7. Parsley or watercress can be used as a garnish, if desired.

Stir-Fried Gingered Beef

Serves 3 to 4

1 pound flank steak
⅓ cup water
¼ cup sherry
2 tablespoons soy sauce
2 tablespoons peanut oil
1 large clove garlic, minced

1 teaspoon shredded ginger root
3 cups sliced radishes
1 cup diagonally-sliced green onions
1 can (10½ ounces) condensed
  golden mushroom soup
hot cooked rice

1. Place steak in freezer for 1 hour to firm for easier slicing. Start at narrow end of steak and slice diagonally across the grain in very thin slices.
2. Combine water, sherry, and soy sauce; add steak and marinate 1 hour.
3. Pour oil in electric wok; preheat, uncovered, at medium heat about 2 minutes.
4. Add steak, marinade, garlic and ginger; cook in oil about 5 minutes, stirring constantly.
5. Push mixture up the side; add radishes, green onions and soup. Cook 3 minutes, stirring constantly.
6. Serve over hot cooked rice.

NOTE: Substitute 10-inch skillet for electric wok. After steak is cooked, push meat to the side. Add radishes, green onions and soup; proceed as above.

Stuffed Flank Steak, Swiss Style

Serves 6

1 flank steak, weighing 1½
  to 2 pounds
salt
pepper
¼ cup minced onion
2 apples, peeled, cored and
  sliced
8 pitted prunes

2 tablespoons corn oil
1 cup water
1 tablespoon instant beef bouillon
1½ cups apple juice
2 tablespoons cornstarch
2 tablespoons instant coffee
  powder
1 tablespoon brown sugar

¼ teaspoon onion powder

1. Trim excess fat and membrane from steak; score both sides and sprinkle with salt and pepper. Pound both sides with meat mallet.
2. Sprinkle one side with onion; arrange apples and prunes in center across short side of steak. Fold in thirds and tie securely.
3. Heat oil in Dutch oven over medium heat; add steak and brown on all sides.
4. Reduce heat; add water and instant bouillon. Cover and simmer 1 hour, or until meat is fork-tender.
5. Remove meat; keep warm.
6. Gradually stir apple juice into cornstarch and coffee until smooth; stir in pan juices.
7. Stir in 1 teaspoon salt, brown sugar and onion powder; cook over medium heat, stirring constantly, until mixture thickens and comes to a boil.
8. Serve gravy over meat.

Steak Port Antonio

Serves 4

¼ cup dark rum
1 tablespoon chopped shallots
½ cup butter or margarine
2 teaspoons fresh lime juice

½ teaspoon Tabasco sauce
1 tablespoon chopped parsley
4 shell steaks or boneless rib
   steaks, about 6 ounces each

1. Combine rum and shallots in small saucepan; bring to a boil.
2. Reduce heat and simmer 2 minutes.
3. Stir in butter, lime juice, Tabasco and parsley.
4. Place shell steaks under preheated broiler 6 inches from heat; brush with rum butter and broil 4 minutes.
5. Turn steaks; brush again and broil 4 minutes longer.
6. Serve with additional rum butter and Tabasco sauce, if desired.

Ripe Olive Cheeseburgers
with Bean Sprout Salad

Serves 6

¾ cup canned pitted California
   ripe olives
2 cups grated Swiss cheese
¼ cup real mayonnaise
4 teaspoons prepared yellow mustard
½ teaspoon paprika
2 teaspoons chopped parsley
1¼ pounds lean ground beef
1½ teaspoons seasoned salt

1 teaspoon onion powder
⅛ teaspoon pepper
6 whole wheat English muffins,
   split
soft butter
6 thin slices tomato
6 thin slices onion
Bean Sprout Salad
avocado slices (optional garnish)

1. Drain olives; coarsely chop and mix with cheese, mayonnaise, mustard, paprika and parsley. Set aside.
2. Preheat broiler.
3. Mix beef with seasoned salt, onion powder and pepper; shape into 6 patties.
4. Place patties on broiler rack 3 inches from heat; broil to desired degree of doneness.
5. Place a meat patty on each of 6 buttered muffin halves; top each with ⅓ cup of cheese mixture.
6. Return to broiler and broil until cheese melts and bubbles, about 1 to 2 minutes.
7. Arrange tomato and onion slices on remaining toasted muffin halves.
8. For serving, place Bean Sprout Salad in lettuce cups; garnish plate with avocado slices and an additional whole ripe olive, if desired.

Bean Sprout Salad

2 cups bean sprouts
¼ cup bottled Italian dressing

2 tablespoons diced pimiento
6 lettuce cups

1. Place bean sprouts in bowl; add Italian dressing and pimiento, tossing together lightly.
2. Serve in lettuce cups with Ripe Olive Cheeseburgers.

Steak Caribbean

Serves 6 to 8

⅓ cup fresh orange juice
¼ cup dry red wine
2 tablespoons vegetable oil
1 tablespoon vinegar
2 cloves garlic, crushed

1½ teaspoons salt
½ teaspoon Tabasco sauce
½ teaspoon turmeric
½ teaspoon ground ginger
½ teaspoon dry mustard

3 pounds London broil

1. Combine orange juice, wine, oil, vinegar, garlic, salt, Tabasco, turmeric, ginger and mustard; mix well.
2. Place steak in a shallow, flat dish; cover with marinade and marinate at room temperature 2 hours, turning occasionally.
3. Remove steak from marinade; broil to desired degree of doneness, basting with marinade.
4. Serve remaining marinade with meat. If desired, serve with additional Tabasco sauce.

Italian Beef Roll

Serves 6

2 pounds round steak, cut ½ inch thick
1 teaspoon salt
½ teaspoon pepper
garlic juice (optional)
2 to 3 tablespoons flour
2 to 3 tablespoons olive oil

2 onions, minced
½ pound diced salami
3 hard-cooked eggs, cut up
1 cup grated Cheddar cheese
½ cup water or beef stock
1 can tomato sauce

½ cup dry red wine (optional)

1. Pound meat thoroughly with tenderizer; rub with salt and pepper (garlic fanciers may add a bit of garlic juice here); dust with flour.
2. Using a deep skillet, Dutch oven or heavy pan, as for a pot roast, heat olive oil over a medium flame.
3. While oil heats, stuff round steak with onions, salami, hard-cooked eggs and grated cheese; roll and tie with kitchen cord.
4. Increase flame and braise beef roll until brown on all sides; pour ½ cup water over meat.
5. Add tomato sauce; cook in tightly-covered pan over low flame 1½ hours, turning occasionally. (Add additional liquid as necessary, to prevent sticking.)
6. When meat has cooked 1½ hours, remove cover and add ½ cup wine, if desired.
7. Thicken with 1 tablespoon flour; cover and cook 20 minutes, lacing with additional wine as mixture thickens.
8. Taste to correct seasonings.

Sizzle Hamburgers

Serves 4 to 5

1 tablespoon butter or margarine
1 tablespoon Worcestershire sauce
pepper to taste

4 or 5 ground beef patties
salt to taste

1. Melt butter with Worcestershire sauce in skillet.
2. Add ground beef patties; cook until done.
3. Season to taste with salt and pepper.

MICROCOOK SIZZLE BURGERS: Preheat browning skillet on HIGH 5 minutes; add Worcestershire. Arrange ground beef patties in skillet. Microcook on HIGH 5 minutes. Turn patties; cook 1 to 2 minutes longer.

Ripe Olive-Centered Picnic Loaf

Serves 6 to 8

oil
1¼ cups soft bread crumbs
¾ cup milk
1 beef bouillon cube, crushed
1 teaspoon salt
¼ teaspoon seasoned pepper
½ teaspoon basil
¼ teaspoon thyme
2 eggs

1 cup chopped onion
¾ cup grated potato, undrained
2 pounds ground lean beef
1½ cups canned pitted California
ripe olives
2 cups grated Monterey Jack
or muenster cheese
¼ cup diced pimiento
¼ cup chopped parsley

1. Prepare a 9 x 5 x 2¾-inch loaf pan by folding an 18-inch length of waxed paper to width of bottom of pan; fit into pan so ends of paper extend above sides of pan.
2. Grease waxed paper and sides of pan with oil.
3. Mix together crumbs, milk, bouillon cube, salt, pepper, basil, thyme and eggs; let stand for 1 minute.
4. Add onion, potato and beef; mix well.
5. Divide mixture in half; pack one-half into loaf pan.
6. Mix ripe olives with cheese, pimiento and parsley; pack onto meat in pan.
7. Top with remaining meat mixture.
8. Loosen sides with spatula and invert loaf pan onto baking sheet; remove pan and lift off paper.
9. Bake in preheated 350° F. oven 1 hour. Serve warm or cold.

Beef Elegante over Rice

Serves 6

1½ pounds round steak, thinly sliced
½ cup seasoned flour
3 tablespoons corn oil
1 cup chopped onions
¼ cup dry red wine

1¾ cups beef broth
1 can (4 ounces) sliced mushrooms
  with liquid
3 cups hot cooked rice
tomato wedges (for garnish)

fresh parsley (for garnish)

1. Have butcher tenderize steak; cut into 1-inch strips.
2. Coat steaks with seasoned flour; brown in oil.
3. Add onions and cook 2 to 3 minutes longer.
4. Stir in wine, broth, and mushrooms with liquid; bring to a boil.
5. Cover, reduce heat, and simmer 20 to 30 minutes, or until tender.
6. Serve over rice; garnish with tomato wedges and fresh parsley.

NOTE: *Beef broth may be substituted for wine.*

Mini Meat Loaves

Makes 6 mini loaves

1 pound ground beef or ¾ pound
  ground beef and ¼ pound ground
  sausage
⅓ cup quick oats, uncooked
1 egg, slightly beaten
2 tablespoons freshly squeezed
  lemon juice

2 tablespoons grated onion
½ teaspoon salt
¼ teaspoon oregano leaves, crushed
¼ teaspoon thyme leaves, crushed
3 tablespoons catsup
1 tablespoon brown sugar
1 teaspoon fresh grated lemon peel

1 teaspoon dry mustard

1. Cut six 6-inch circles of foil; press foil into 2½ x 1¼-inch muffin cups, letting foil extend above side of cups.
2. In large bowl, thoroughly combine ground beef, oats, egg, lemon juice, onion, salt, oregano and thyme; shape into six balls.
3. Press balls into foil-lined muffin cups; bake in preheated 375° F. oven 25 minutes.
4. Meanwhile, to make sauce, combine catsup, brown sugar, lemon peel and dry mustard; spoon sauce on top of baked meat loaves; bake 5 minutes longer.
5. Remove from foil and serve.

Brisket in Foil

Serves 6

3 to 4 pounds beef brisket
½ envelope onion soup mix
pepper

½ cup dry red wine
8 carrots
4 potatoes

1. Trim excess fat from brisket.
2. Place meat on large sheet of heavy foil in shallow roasting pan; sprinkle with onion soup mix and pepper. Pour wine around meat.
3. Peel carrots and potatoes; cut into halves or serving-size pieces and arrange around meat.
4. Wrap foil to form an airtight package, but allowing space for gravy to form; bake in preheated 325° F. oven 3 to 4 hours.
5. Slice meat across grain; serve with pan juices and vegetables.

Beef Brisket with Jardinere Sauce

Serves 4

1½ pounds lean beef brisket
2 tablespoons corn oil
½ cup coarsely chopped onion
½ cup coarsely chopped carrots
½ cup coarsely chopped celery

2 cloves garlic, minced or
pressed
1½ cups low-sodium beef bouillon
1 tomato, coarsely chopped (1 cup)
¼ teaspoon pepper

1. Trim and discard visible fat from brisket.
2. Heat corn oil in 5-quart Dutch oven over medium heat; add brisket and brown on all sides.
3. Remove meat and set aside.
4. Add onion, carrots, celery and garlic to Dutch oven; cook 2 minutes, stirring frequently.
5. Stir in bouillon, tomato and pepper; return brisket, cover and bring to a boil.
6. Reduce heat and simmer 50 to 60 minutes, or until brisket is tender.
7. Remove brisket; cover and refrigerate.
8. Cover and refrigerate vegetable mixture several hours, or overnight.
9. Remove any surface fat from vegetable mixture; place mixture in blender, cover, and blend on medium speed 15 seconds, or until puréed.
10. Place vegetable mixture in large skillet; cut brisket into very thin slices and place in vegetable mixture.
11. Cover skillet and reheat gently 5 to 10 minutes, or until heated through.

Frikadeller (Danish Meatballs)

Serves 8

1 pound ground beef
½ pound ground veal
3 medium potatoes, cooked
   and mashed
1 medium onion, minced

sifted flour
1 egg, beaten
2 to 4 tablespoons milk
2½ teaspoons salt
¼ teaspoon white pepper

lard (for deep-fat frying)

1. Combine ground beef and veal, mashed potatoes and onion; add 1½ cups flour and mix well.
2. Add egg, milk, salt and pepper; stir until well blended.
3. Shape into 32 balls, using about 2 tablespoons mixture for each ball; roll balls in additional flour.
4. Fry in deep hot lard (350° F.) 5 minutes, or until browned.
5. Drain and serve.

Sauerkraut 'n' Meatballs

Serves 8 to 10

¼ pound bacon
water
2 cans (27 ounces each) sauerkraut, squeezed dry
3 cups chicken broth
1 cup dry white wine
1 bay leaf
salt
pepper
2 pounds lean ground beef

2 eggs, lightly beaten
½ cup bread crumbs
¼ cup diced onion
¾ teaspoon dried tarragon
1 garlic clove, minced
½ teaspoon Worcestershire sauce
½ cup bacon drippings
3 cups tart apples, peeled and
   thinly sliced
1 pint dairy sour cream

1. Simmer bacon in water to cover for 10 minutes; drain and dice.
2. Combine bacon, sauerkraut, 2 cups broth, wine and bay leaf in heavy Dutch oven; bring to a boil.
3. Cover and simmer gently 1 hour, adding more water or broth, if necessary; season to taste with salt and pepper.
4. Meanwhile, combine ground beef, eggs, bread crumbs, onions, tarragon, garlic, 1 teaspoon salt, Worcestershire and ½ teaspoon pepper; mix lightly with hands. Form into 18 to 24 meatballs.
5. Heat bacon drippings in large heavy skillet; add meatballs and brown quickly on all sides.
6. Alternate layers of sauerkraut, apples and meatballs in Dutch oven or large heavy casserole, ending with sauerkraut.
7. Add remaining 1 cup broth; cover and simmer 1 hour.
8. Just before serving, top with dollops of sour cream.

Spicy Beef Pot Roast

Serves 6

¼ teaspoon marjoram
2 bay leaves, crushed
1 clove garlic, crushed
1 green pepper, minced
1 small onion, minced
¼ cup olive oil

3 to 4 pounds beef rump
1 can (16 ounces) tomatoes with
  liquid
¼ teaspoon cinnamon
⅛ teaspoon cloves
2 teaspoons salt

2 cups red wine or orange juice

1. Combine and mash to a paste herbs, garlic, green pepper, onion and olive oil; rub into beef and let stand 1 hour.
2. Brown meat in large saucepan.
3. Add remaining ingredients; cover and simmer gently 3 to 4 hours, or until very tender.
4. Thicken gravy, if desired.

Swedish Pot Roast

Serves 6 to 8

1 large onion, sliced
1 tablespoon corn oil
4 pounds beef chuck or rump
  roast
salt to taste
¾ cup dry red wine

water
1 tablespoon Worcestershire
  sauce
1 teaspoon caraway seed
¼ cup flour
½ cup dairy sour cream

1. Cook onion in oil in Dutch oven until soft; remove and reserve.
2. Brown roast in same pan; season with salt.
3. Add onions, wine, ¾ cup water, Worcestershire and caraway seed; cover tightly and simmer, turning occasionally, 2½ to 3 hours, or until tender.
4. Remove meat to heated platter; keep warm.
5. Skim fat from pan drippings; add enough water to make 1½ cups liquid.
6. Mix flour with ½ cup water to form a smooth paste; stir into pan liquid and heat, stirring, until gravy comes to a boil and thickens.
7. Reduce heat; stir in sour cream and additional salt to taste, if desired.

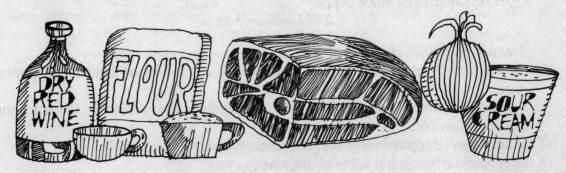

Chinese Pot Roast

Serves 6 to 8

3 to 4 pounds beef arm or blade
   pot roast
3 tablespoons lard or drippings

¼ teaspoon pepper
1 tablespoon soy sauce
⅓ cup water

2 quarts shredded cabbage

1. Brown meat on all sides in lard; pour off drippings.
2. Add pepper, soy sauce and water; cover tightly and cook slowly 3 hours, or until meat is tender.
3. Add cabbage; steam 7 minutes. Thicken cooking liquid for gravy, if desired.

Hearty Pot Roast

Serves 6 to 8

¼ cup corn oil
4 to 5 pounds second-cut, bone-in
   chuck roast
2 medium onions, sliced
3 cups beef bouillon
1 teaspoon salt

1 teaspoon pepper
2 bay leaves
1 pound carrots, cut in 2-inch
   pieces
1 pound small white onions
3 tablespoons cornstarch

¼ cup water

1. Heat corn oil in Dutch oven over medium heat; add roast and brown on all sides.
2. Add onions, bouillon, salt, pepper and bay leaves; cover and bring to a boil.
3. Reduce heat and simmer 2 hours.
4. Add carrots and onions; continue cooking 30 minutes, or until meat and vegetables are tender.
5. Remove meat and vegetables to platter; keep warm.
6. Stir together cornstarch and water until smooth; stir into juice in Dutch oven. Bring to a boil, stirring constantly over medium heat; boil 1 minute. Serve over meat.

San Joaquin Oven Roast

Serves 6

4 pounds bone-in chuck roast or
   steak
2 teaspoons salt
¼ teaspoon ground black pepper

¾ teaspoon marjoram leaves,
   crumbled
¼ cup freeze-dried shallots
water

2 tablespoons flour

1. Sprinkle both sides of roast with salt, black pepper and marjoram.
2. Place in roasting pan in preheated 500° F. oven; brown on both sides, turning once, 30 to 40 minutes.
3. Sprinkle shallots over top of meat; cover and reduce heat to 350° F. Cook 1 hour, or until tender.
4. Measure pan drippings for gravy; add enough water to measure 2 cups.
5. Blend in flour; cook and stir until thickened.

Easy Beef Wellington
with Bearnaise Sauce

Serves 8 to 10

4 pounds beef tenderloin,
    evenly shaped
1 cup fresh mushrooms, cleaned
    and minced
2 tablespoons minced onion
1 tablespoon sweet butter
1 tablespoon olive or corn oil

½ cup liver pâte (available
    at gourmet shop or delicatessen)
1 tablespoon minced fresh parsley
prepared crust (enough for 4
    nine-inch pie crusts)
water
1 egg white

Bearnaise Sauce

1. Place tenderloin, fat-side up, on rack in shallow roasting pan; roast in preheated 450° F. oven 25 minutes, or until meat thermometer registers 130° F.
2. Remove meat from oven; cool.
3. Meanwhile, sauté mushrooms and onion in butter and olive oil; blend in pâté and parsley, blending well.
4. Roll pastry on lightly floured board into two 12 x 8-inch rectangles; spread half of pâté mixture evenly on each rectangle, leaving 1-inch margin on all sides.
5. Center tenderloin, fat-side up, on first rectangle so pâté side is inside; cover with remaining rectangle with pâté side next to meat.
6. Moisten edges of pastry with water; overlap and press to securely seal edges. (Roll out remaining dough and cut decorative shapes for top.)
7. Add 1 tablespoon water to egg white for egg wash; beat lightly and spread evenly over entire top of pastry.
8. Bake in preheated 400° F. oven 40 minutes, or until pastry is golden.
9. Slice and serve with Bearnaise Sauce.

Bearnaise Sauce

3 shallots, chopped, or
    3 tablespoons chopped onion
1 sprig parsley
½ teaspoon dried tarragon
½ teaspoon dried chervil

¼ cup red wine vinegar
2 tablespoons water
4 egg yolks
¼ cup sweet butter, softened
salt

cayenne pepper

1. Combine shallots, parsley, tarragon, chervil and vinegar in water; bring to a boil and simmer 3 minutes.
2. Drain. Add liquid, a few drops at a time, to egg yolks in top of double boiler, stirring constantly with wire whisk.
3. Cook over hot water, stirring constantly, until mixture thickens.
4. Add butter, 1 tablespoon at a time, blending well after each addition.
5. Season to taste with salt and cayenne. Serve with Beef Wellington.

Prime Rib Roast

Cooking Instructions

Season roast with salt and pepper.

Place fat-side up in open roasting pan.

Insert meat thermometer into the thickest part; make sure it does not rest on bone or fat. Do not add water. Do not cover or wrap in foil.

Roast in 325° F. oven to desired doneness. The meat thermometer will register 140°F. for rare; 160°F. for medium; 170°F. for well done.

Roasts are more easily carved if permitted to "set" in warm place 15 to 20 minutes after removal from oven before carving. Roasts continue to cook after removal from oven, so it is best to remove the roast when thermometer registers about 5° F. below the temperature of doneness desired.

Timetable For Roasting

A roast 4 to 6 pounds, allow 26 to 32 minutes per pound for rare.
A roast 4 to 6 pounds, allow 34 to 38 minutes per pound for medium.
A roast 4 to 6 pounds, allow 40 to 42 minutes per pound for well done.

A roast 6 to 8 pounds, allow 23 to 25 minutes per pound for rare.
A roast 6 to 8 pounds, allow 27 to 30 minutes per pound for medium.
A roast 6 to 8 pounds, allow 32 to 35 minutes per pound for well done.

Standing Rib Roast with Yorkshire Pudding

For the Roast

1. Place rib roast, rib ends down, on a rack in open roasting pan.
2. Roast in preheated 300° F. oven to desired doneness: 18 to 20 minutes per pound for rare, 22 to 25 minutes for medium and 27 to 30 minutes for well done.

Yorkshire Pudding

Serves 6 to 8

1 cup sifted all-purpose flour   1 cup milk
1 teaspoon salt   2 eggs
3 tablespoons beef drippings

1. Sift together flour and salt; add milk gradually, stirring to form a smooth paste.
2. Beat eggs; add to flour mixture.
3. Remove roast from oven; measure off 3 tablespoons drippings from pan and pour into batter.
4. Bake in moderately hot oven (400° F.) 30 to 40 minutes.
5. Cut into squares and serve around meat.

NOTE: Pudding gets puffy if container is oiled and put into a hot oven before adding batter.

Steak au Poivre
(Pepper Steak)

Serves 6 to 8

1 to 2 tablespoons coarsely
  ground black pepper
4 pounds boned sirloin steak,
  2 inches thick

1 teaspoon salt
½ cup dry red wine

1. Rub black pepper into both sides of steak; let stand at room temperature for ½ hour.
2. Lightly grease large heavy skillet; heat until hot.
3. Sprinkle both sides of steak with salt; place in skillet and cook 8 to 10 minutes on each side, or until done as desired.
4. Remove meat to serving platter.
5. Add wine to skillet; cook and stir one minute.
6. Pour sauce over steak; slice and serve.

Grilled T-Bone Steaks

Serves 2 to 3

2 beef loin T-bone or sirloin
  steaks, cut 1 inch thick
½ cup soy sauce
¼ cup dry white wine

2 tablespoons sugar
½ teaspoon ginger
¼ teaspoon dry mustard
¼ teaspoon onion powder

⅛ teaspoon garlic powder

1. Place steaks in shallow pan.
2. Combine remaining ingredients; pour over steaks and marinate 20 minutes.
3. Remove steaks from marinade and place on grill 6 inches from coals; cook to desired doneness, turning and brushing occasionally with marinade.

Barbecued Ribs Western

Serves 10

10 pounds beef spareribs,
  parboiled and separated
1 can (12 ounces) vegetable
  juice cocktail
1 cup chili sauce
1 cup catsup
½ cup fresh lemon juice

½ cup prepared yellow mustard
¼ cup corn oil
3 tablespoons Worcestershire sauce
3 tablespoons brown sugar
1 tablespoon grated lemon peel
1 teaspoon salt
⅛ teaspoon pepper

1. Combine remaining ingredients in saucepan; bring to a boil and cook, uncovered, 5 to 6 minutes.
2. Dip ribs into sauce and grill or roast 40 to 45 minutes, or until tender, basting frequently and turning to brown evenly.

NOTE: This sauce is also excellent with preroasted beef ribs.

Broiled Steak with Mushroom Wine Sauce

Serves 6

2 tablespoons margarine
¼ pound mushrooms, thinly sliced
2 tablespoons finely chopped onion
1 clove garlic, crushed
2 teaspoons flour

¼ teaspoon salt
generous dash pepper
2 tablespoons tomato paste
½ cup dry red wine
¼ cup water

2 pounds boneless sirloin steak

1. Melt margarine in small saucepan over medium heat. Add mushrooms, onion and garlic; sauté until onion is transparent, stirring frequently.
2. Remove from heat; stir in flour, salt, pepper and tomato paste.
3. Blend in wine and water; bring to a boil, stirring frequently.
4. Cover, reduce heat, and simmer 20 minutes.
5. Meanwhile, broil steak to desired doneness.
6. Serve steak with sauce.

Sirloin Steak Nectarine Sukiyaki

Serves 6 to 8

2 pounds sirloin steak (one piece)
2 large onions
6 to 8 green onions
¼ pound mushrooms
1 can (5 ounces) bamboo shoots

3 or 4 fresh California nectarines
½ cup soy sauce
2 tablespoons sugar
½ cup condensed beef broth
hot cooked rice

1. Cut steak crosswise into thin slices, saving fat.
2. Cut onions into thin wedges; slice green onions, including tops, into 2-inch lengths.
3. Slice mushrooms and bamboo shoots.
4. Slice nectarines to make 2 cups.
5. Grease skillet by rendering steak fat. Remove fat; brown beef quickly.
6. Add sliced vegetables.
7. Combine soy sauce, sugar and broth; add to meat along with nectarines. Simmer 5 minutes.
8. Serve over hot cooked rice.

Sizzling Summer Steak, Barbecue Style

Serves 4 to 6

⅔ cup teriyaki sauce
2 pounds sirloin steak

½ cup water
1 teaspoon cornstarch

1 tablespoon sugar

1. Pour teriyaki sauce over steak in shallow pan; marinate 15 to 20 minutes.
2. Remove steak from marinade; place on grill 4 to 5 inches from heat. Cook to desired doneness.
3. Meanwhile, blend ½ cup marinade with remaining ingredients; thicken over medium heat, stirring constantly. Serve with steak.

Short Ribs & Gravy

Serves 4

4 pounds beef short ribs
1 can (10½ ounces) beef broth
1 teaspoon salt
¼ teaspoon pepper
¼ teaspoon thyme
1 bay leaf
1 cup sliced onion

4 celery tops
4 carrots, pared
1 cup diced turnips or rutabaga
2 tablespoons flour
1 cup undiluted evaporated milk
1 teaspoon original Worcester-
    shire sauce

1. Place ribs, meat-side down, in 13 x 9 x 2-inch baking dish; bake, uncovered, in preheated 425° F. oven 45 minutes.
2. Drain off fat; add broth, salt, pepper, thyme, bay leaf, onion and celery tops.
3. Cover dish with foil, reduce oven temperature to 350° F., and continue baking for 1 hour and 15 minutes, or until meat is tender.
4. Slice carrots lengthwise; add carrots and turnips for the last 30 minutes of baking time.
5. Remove meat and vegetables; keep warm. Discard celery tops and bay leaf.
6. Reserve 1 cup meat juice; slowly stir juice into flour.
7. Add evaporated milk and Worcestershire sauce; cook over medium heat until thick, stirring constantly.
8. Serve gravy with meat and vegetables.

Yogurt Stroganoff

Serves 4

1½ pounds lean beef stew
3 tablespoons flour
1 teaspoon salt
⅛ teaspoon pepper
2 tablespoons butter
1 can (2 ounces) mushroom stems
    and pieces, undrained

1½ cups sliced onions
1 cup water
3 tablespoons catsup
1 teaspoon original Worcester-
    shire sauce
½ teaspoon garlic powder
½ pint plain yogurt

buttered poppy seed noodles or rice

1. Cut beef into 1-inch cubes; roll in flour mixed with salt and pepper.
2. Brown beef in butter, a few pieces at a time, over medium-high heat.
3. Return all beef to skillet; add liquid drained from mushrooms, onions, water, catsup, Worcestershire sauce and garlic powder. Do not stir, but cover and bring to a boil.
4. Reduce heat and simmer, stirring occasionally, about 1 hour, or until tender and sauce is thickened.
5. Just before serving, stir yogurt until smooth; add yogurt, along with mushrooms, to beef. Heat 1 or 2 minutes.
6. Serve over buttered poppy seed noodles or rice.

NOTE: Buttermilk may be used in place of yogurt.

Texas Beef Short Ribs

Serves 4

1 cup tomato juice
½ cup vinegar
3 tablespoons chili powder
1 tablespoon brown sugar

1 tablespoon onion powder
1½ teaspoons salt
½ teaspoon oregano leaves
½ teaspoon garlic powder

3 pounds lean beef short ribs

1. Combine all ingredients except meat; blend well.
2. Place meat in tight-fitting bowl; pour marinade over meat, cover or seal, and refrigerate 10 hours, or longer.
3. Remove meat and place on rack in a baking pan; bake in preheated 400° F. oven for 1½ hours, or until done, turning and basting frequently with marinade.

Beef Carbonnade
(Beef Cooked in Beer)

Serves 6

½ cup onion flakes
⅓ cup water
2½ pounds boneless lean beef
  stew meat
⅓ cup flour
4 tablespoons oil

1 can (12 fluid ounces) beer
2 teaspoons salt
¼ teaspoon garlic powder
¼ teaspoon ground nutmeg
¼ teaspoon ground thyme
¼ teaspoon ground black pepper

1. Rehydrate onion flakes in water 10 minutes.
2. Cut beef into 2-inch cubes; dredge with flour and set aside.
3. Heat oil in a Dutch oven; add beef cubes and brown on all sides.
4. Add onion flakes; sauté 5 minutes.
5. Stir in remaining ingredients; cover, reduce heat, and simmer 1½ hours or until meat is tender.

Creamed Sweetbread Olivero

Makes 3 cups

1 quart water
1 teaspoon salt
1 tablespoon lemon juice
1 pound sweetbreads
½ cup sliced onion
¼ teaspoon grated fresh garlic
  or 2 to 3 drops garlic juice

2 tablespoons butter or margarine
1 can (10¾ ounces) condensed
  cream of mushroom soup
⅓ cup milk
⅓ cup chopped canned tomatoes
¼ cup sliced stuffed olives
hot cooked rice

1. Combine water, salt and lemon juice in saucepan; bring to a boil.
2. Add sweetbreads; cover and cook over low heat 20 minutes.
3. Drain; remove membrane and cut sweetbreads into cubes.
4. Brown sweetbreads, onion and garlic in butter in saucepan until onion is tender.
5. Add soup, milk, tomatoes and olives; heat, stirring occasionally.
6. Serve over hot cooked rice.

Barbecued Steak 'n' Sweetbreads with Tarragon Butter

Serves 6

1 pound sweetbreads
1 quart water
1 tablespoon fresh lemon juice
1 teaspoon salt

4 strips bacon, partially cooked
1 pound boneless beef sirloin or chuck, cut in 1½-inch chunks
Tarragon Butter

1. Cover sweetbreads with water; add lemon juice and salt.
2. Heat to a boil; simmer 15 minutes and drain.
3. Run cold water over sweetbreads to cool them; drain and pull off any visible white membrane. Cut into 1 to 1½-inch chunks.
4. Cut partially cooked bacon into 1-inch lengths.
5. Thread beef cubes, bacon and sweetbreads on skewers; brush with Tarragon Butter.
6. Cook over hot coals about 10 minutes, or until done as desired, brushing occasionally with Tarragon Butter as beef cooks.
7. Pass remaining Tarragon Butter on side.

Tarragon Butter

½ cup sweet butter
1 tablespoon fresh lemon juice
1 tablespoon minced parsley

1 teaspoon grated lemon peel
¼ teaspoon onion salt
½ teaspoon crumbled tarragon

1. Combine butter, lemon juice, parsley, lemon peel, onion salt and tarragon.
2. Heat briefly until butter melts.

Tongue Mexicano

Serves 6

2 to 3 pounds fresh or smoked beef tongue
2 tablespoons whole pickling spice
¼ cup olive oil
1 small onion, chopped
1 clove garlic, pressed
4 peeled, chopped ripe tomatoes

⅓ cup sherry
1 tablespoon quava jelly
4 teaspoons Angostura aromatic bitters
salt to taste
freshly ground black pepper to taste

1. Simmer smoked tongue in water to cover until tongue is tender, about 2 to 3 hours. (Fresh tongue should be cooked in water to cover with pickling spices added until tongue is cooked, about 2 to 3 hours.)
2. Heat olive oil; sauté onion and garlic in oil until soft.
3. Add tomatoes, sherry, jelly and Angostura bitters; simmer 5 minutes.
4. Add salt and pepper to taste.
5. Remove skin and gristle from tongue; slice thinly.
6. Serve sliced tongue with sauce spooned over all.

Savory London Broil

Serves 4 to 6

1 to 1¾ pounds beef flank steak	2 tablespoons catsup
1 small onion, chopped	1 tablespoon brown sugar
2 tablespoons vinegar	2 tablespoons salad oil
¼ cup water	1 teaspoon salt

½ teaspoon Tabasco sauce

1. Place flank steak and onion in shallow utility dish.
2. Combine vinegar, water, catsup, brown sugar, salad oil, salt and hot sauce; mix thoroughly and pour over steak.
3. Turn steak, cover dish with foil, and marinate in refrigerator 12 to 24 hours.
4. Remove steak from marinade and place on rack in broiling pan; broil 3 to 4 inches from heat 5 minutes. Turn steak, brush with marinade, and broil second side 5 minutes, or to desired degree of doneness.
5. Carve steak diagonally and across the grain into very thin slices.

Steak & Kidney Pie

Serves 8

2 beef kidneys	1 teaspoon salt
2 pounds shoulder or round steak, cut into 1-inch cubes	3 tablespoons flour
3 tablespoons corn oil	¾ cup plus 2 teaspoons water
2 cups chopped onions	½ pound sliced mushrooms
1 cup diced celery	2 tablespoons chopped parsley
¼ cup original Worcester- shire sauce	1 package (10 ounces) pie crust mix
	1 tablespoon fresh lemon juice
	1 egg yolk

1. Split kidneys open; remove all fat and white veins. Soak in cold water to cover for 30 minutes. Drain and cut into 1-inch cubes.
2. Brown kidneys and steak in corn oil in a Dutch oven.
3. Add onions, celery, Worcestershire and salt; cook, uncovered, 10 minutes, stirring frequently. Cover and simmer 1 hour, or until meat is tender.
4. Mix flour with ¾ cup water; gradually stir into meat mixture.
5. Add mushrooms and parsley; cook until gravy is thickened.
6. Turn into 1½-quart ovenproof casserole; set aside.
7. Prepare pastry according to package directions, using lemon juice as part of water.
8. Roll ⅛ inch thick to fit top of casserole; trim and flute edges.
9. Re-roll pastry trimmings; cut out leaf and stem design and arrange on top of pastry. Make cuts in pastry for steam to escape.
10. Combine egg yolk with 2 teaspoons water; brush over pastry.
11. Bake in preheated 425° F. oven 20 minutes; reduce temperature to 350° F. and bake 20 minutes longer, or until pastry is nicely browned.

NOTE: If desired, kidneys may be omitted. In their place, use a total of 3 pounds beef.

Pepper Steak au Rhum

Serves 6

1 tablespoon coarsely-ground pepper	4 tablespoons butter
3 pounds sirloin steak, cut 1½ inches thick	2 tablespoons 151 proof rum

1. Rub pepper into both sides of sirloin steak; let stand several hours.
2. Heat butter in a skillet (an electric skillet set at 350° F. may be used at table) for 8 minutes on each side for rare.
3. Add rum; set aflame.
4. When flame has died out (because of the butter, the blaze will be high), spoon sauce over steak, scraping up pan drippings.
5. Carve at a 45-degree angle in thin slices.

Garlicky Sprout Kabobs

Serves 4

1 pint Brussels sprouts	2 onions
boiling salted water	3 cloves fresh garlic
1 pound beef sirloin	1 cup Italian dressing

1 teaspoon soy sauce

1. Cook sprouts, covered, in a little boiling salted water until tender, 5 to 10 minutes.
2. Cut beef into 1-inch cubes; cut onions into wedges.
3. Crush garlic with butt end of a knife handle; combine garlic, dressing and soy sauce.
4. Marinate sprouts, beef and onion in dressing mixture for 1 to 2 hours; thread on skewers, alternating ingredients.
5. Broil 3 to 4 inches from heat until beef is done.
6. Heat marinade and serve with kabobs, if desired.

Steak Diane

Serves 4

2 pounds boneless sirloin, ½ inch thick	1 tablespoon chopped chives
½ teaspoon dry mustard	1 tablespoon fresh lemon juice
¼ teaspoon salt	1 teaspoon original Worcester- shire sauce
⅛ teaspoon freshly ground pepper	3 tablespoons Cognac, heated just to boiling
2 tablespoons margarine	

1. Wipe steak with paper towel to remove moisture.
2. Mix together dry mustard, salt and pepper; sprinkle over one side of steak, then rub in.
3. Melt margarine in electric skillet on high setting; brown steak well on each side.
4. Sprinkle on chives, lemon juice and Worcestershire.
5. Pour heated Cognac over steak; ignite.
6. When flame goes out, transfer steak to serving platter; spoon pan juices over meat and serve.

Breast of Lamb with Fruited Rice Stuffing

Serves 6

2 tablespoons corn oil
4 pounds breast of lamb, cut
  into serving-size pieces and
  trimmed of fat
salt
pepper
3 cups cooked rice
½ cup chopped apricots or prunes

1 cup diced green apple
⅓ cup chopped green onions
  and tops
1 tablespoon fresh lemon juice
½ cup sunflower seeds
½ cup dry white wine
1 cup water
apple sections (for garnish)

1. Heat pressure cooker; add oil and brown pieces of lamb breast on both sides over medium heat.
2. Remove lamb; sprinkle both sides with salt and pepper.
3. Combine in 1-quart bowl rice, apricots or prunes, diced apple, onions, lemon juice and sunflower seeds.
4. Place 2 pieces of lamb breast, cavity-side up, in bottom of pressure cooker; fill each with rice mixture.
5. Make third layer of lamb and rice. (Do not fill cooker over ⅔ full.)
6. Pour wine and water down *side* of pressure cooker, not over lamb and rice; close cover securely and place pressure regulator on vent pipe. Cook 12 minutes.
7. Cool cooker at once. Carefully remove stuffed lamb breasts to heated plates; pour a little remaining liquid over each.
8. Garnish with apple sections.

NOTE: In high altitudes, for every 1,000 feet over 2,000, increase cooking time by 5%.

Country Lamb Loaf

Serves 10

3 pounds lean ground lamb
1 onion, chopped
1 green pepper, chopped
1¼ cups bread crumbs
1 can (8 ounces) tomato sauce
¾ cup catsup
2 eggs
1 teaspoon salt

1½ teaspoons oregano
1½ teaspoons bottled steak sauce
1 teaspoon original Worcestershire sauce
½ teaspoon pepper
tomato, onion and green pepper slices
  (for garnish)

1. Combine lamb, chopped onion and green pepper, bread crumbs, tomato sauce, ¼ cup catsup, eggs, salt, oregano, steak sauce, Worcestershire and pepper; mix well.
2. Pack mixture into greased 9 x 5 x 3-inch loaf pan, rounding the top; bake in preheated 350° F. oven 1½ hours, or until done.
3. Remove from oven; invert to remove from pan.
4. Turn loaf onto serving platter or wooden board, rounded-side up.
5. Heat remaining ½ cup catsup; spoon over top of loaf.
6. Garnish with tomato, onion and green pepper slices.

Lamb Chili Joes

Serves 4

1 pound ground lamb
1 onion, chopped
½ teaspoon seasoned salt
1 can (8 ounces) tomato sauce
　with herbs

1 can (14½ ounces) kidney beans,
　drained
2 teaspoons chili powder
4 hamburger buns, split and toasted
4 slices American or sharp
　Cheddar cheese

1. Cook lamb in skillet over medium heat until browned, stirring frequently.
2. Add onion, seasoned salt, tomato sauce, kidney beans and chili powder; cook, stirring occasionally, until mixture is hot and bubbly.
3. For each serving, arrange bottom of hamburger bun on plate, pour ¼ of chili-meat mixture over bun, top with cheese, and cover with top of bun.

Grilled Lamb Dinner

Serves 4

⅔ cup corn oil
1 tablespoon vinegar
1 tablespoon grated onion
1 teaspoon seasoned salt

¼ teaspoon ground black pepper
4 Scotch lamb chops or 4 ground
　lamb patties
1 summer squash, sliced

2 tomatoes, sliced

1. Combine oil, vinegar, onion, seasoned salt and pepper; mix well.
2. Brush lamb, squash and tomatoes with oil mixture.
3. Arrange each lamb chop or patty and some squash in center of pieces of heavy-duty aluminum foil; fold foil, using drugstore wrap.
4. Arrange tomato slices in similar foil package.
5. Place lamb and squash on broiler rack or outdoor grill; cook 5 to 7 inches from heat 25 minutes, turning once.
6. Place tomatoes on rack or grill during last 5 minutes of cooking time.

NOTE: Scotch chop is breast of lamb, stuffed with ground lamb and sliced.

Tasty Lamburgers

Serves 4

1 pound ground lamb
¼ cup minced onion
½ cup minced mushrooms
1 egg, beaten

1 teaspoon seasoned salt
¼ teaspoon freshly ground pepper
⅓ cup fine dry bread crumbs
4 toasted hamburger buns

¼ cup chili sauce

1. Combine lamb, onion, mushrooms, egg, seasoned salt, pepper and bread crumbs; mix well.
2. Shape into 4 patties; broil 3 to 4 inches from heat, or grill outdoors 4 to 5 minutes.
3. Turn and grill 4 to 5 minutes.
4. Serve patties on hamburger buns with chili sauce.

Tomato-Cheese Lamburgers

Serves 6

1½ pounds ground lamb
½ cup fine dry bread crumbs
1 egg, beaten

1 teaspoon garlic salt
6 slices Bermuda onion
6 slices tomato

6 slices Swiss cheese

1. Combine lamb, bread crumbs, egg and garlic salt; mix well.
2. Shape into 6 patties; broil 3 to 4 inches from heat, or cook on outdoor grill 4 to 5 minutes.
3. Turn and broil 3 minutes.
4. Top with remaining ingredients; broil 2 minutes.

Try-It, You'll-Like-It Lamburger

Serves 4

1 pound ground lamb
½ cup finely chopped onion
¼ cup sweet pickle relish
1 tablespoon prepared mustard
½ teaspoon garlic salt
½ teaspoon salt

¼ teaspoon freshly ground black pepper
4 hamburger buns, bagels or English muffins, split in two, toasted and buttered

1. Combine lamb, onion, pickle relish, mustard, garlic salt, salt and pepper in mixing bowl; mix well.
2. Divide meat into 4 equal parts; shape into patties.
3. Broil 3 to 4 inches from broiler, or cook on outdoor grill 5 to 6 minutes per side, or until done.
4. Place one cooked patty between each bun, bagel or English muffin.

Scotch Chops with Honey Lemon Sauce

Serves 4

¼ cup butter or margarine, melted
2 tablespoons honey
1 tablespoon minced parsley

1 tablespoon grated lemon rind
4 Scotch lamb chops or 4 ground lamb patties

1. Combine butter, honey, parsley and lemon rind; brush ½ of mixture on lamb.
2. Broil chops 3 to 4 inches from heat 5 to 7 minutes.
3. Turn and brush lamb with remaining honey mixture; broil 5 to 7 minutes, or until desired degree of doneness.

NOTE: Scotch chop is breast of lamb, stuffed with ground lamb and sliced.

Lamb Kidneys

Serves 6

2 small lamb kidneys
¼ cup butter
2 tablespoons olive oil
¼ teaspoon salt
¼ teaspoon oregano

¼ teaspoon marjoram
¼ teaspoon rosemary
¼ teaspoon thyme
½ cup red wine
6 slices buttered toast

1. Quarter kidneys; remove cores.
2. Soak in salted water 30 minutes; drain and pat-dry.
3. Melt butter in skillet; add oil.
4. Add kidneys, salt, oregano, marjoram, rosemary and thyme; cook over medium heat 10 minutes, stirring occasionally. (If necessary, add a small amount of water.)
5. Just before serving, add wine and simmer until hot.
6. Serve over buttered toast.

Broiled Lamb Chop Dinner

Serves 4

1 can (1 pound) potatoes, drained
2 cups sliced cooked carrots
½ cup sliced mushrooms

4 lamb loin chops, cut ¾-inch thick
⅓ cup French dressing
1 teaspoon seasoned salt

1. Arrange potatoes, carrots and mushrooms in bottom of broiler pan.
2. Arrange lamb chops on broiler rack; brush lamb with French dressing.
3. Broil 3 to 4 inches from heat 5 to 7 minutes.
4. Sprinkle with seasoned salt; turn chops.
5. Brush with French dressing; broil 5 to 7 minutes, basting with French dressing during cooking.

Pineapple-Broiled Loin Chops

Serves 4

4 loin lamb chops, cut ¾-inch thick
½ teaspoon salt
½ cup unsweetened pineapple juice

1 teaspoon basil
1 tablespoon red wine vinegar
1 tablespoon grated orange rind

1. Sprinkle lamb with salt.
2. Combine remaining ingredients; mix well.
3. Pour pineapple juice mixture over lamb; chill 1 hour, turning chops occasionally.
4. Remove lamb from juice mixture; reserving juice mixture.
5. Broil lamb 3 to 4 inches from heat, or cook on outdoor grill 5 to 7 minutes per side, or to desired degree of doneness, basting frequently with reserved pineapple juice mixture during roasting.

Mixed Grill

Serves 6

1 pound lamb or pork kidneys
¼ cup butter or margarine
1 tablespoon fresh lemon juice
½ teaspoon marjoram leaves
12 large mushroom caps

3 medium-size tomatoes, halved
6 knockwurst
salt to taste
pepper to taste
2 tablespoons chopped parsley

1. Slice kidneys in half crosswise; remove fat and connective tissue.
2. Melt butter; add lemon juice and marjoram.
3. Place mushrooms, tomatoes, kidneys and knockwurst on grill 5 to 7 inches above medium coals; brush with butter mixture and season with salt and pepper.
4. Grill 10 to 15 minutes, or until vegetables are fork-tender and knockwurst is browned. (Turn knockwurst and kidneys occasionally while grilling.) Kidneys should be slightly pink when done.
5. Remove from grill and serve with parsley sprinkled over vegetables.

NOTE: Veal kidneys cut into chunks may be substituted for lamb or pork, but they are more expensive.

Barbecued Lamb with Snappy Marinade

Serves 4 to 6

⅔ cup tomato juice
3 tablespoons cider vinegar
3 tablespoons chopped onion
2 tablespoons Worcestershire sauce
1 tablespoon brown sugar
¾ teaspoon dry mustard
½ teaspoon salt

1½ pounds boned leg of New Zealand spring lamb, cut into 1-inch cubes
1 zucchini, sliced ½-inch thick
8 small onions, peeled and cut in half
12 small, fresh mushrooms
cherry tomatoes

1. Combine all ingredients except vegetables in small bowl; mix well, cover and refrigerate 4 hours, or overnight.
2. Remove lamb; reserve marinade.
3. Thread lamb on skewers alternately with vegetable pieces; cook on grill over hot coals 15 minutes, turning and brushing often with marinade.

29

Broiled Leg of Lamb
with Gold Sauce

Serves 6 to 8

6- to 7-pound leg of lamb, boned
⅔ cup olive oil
6 tablespoons Florida frozen con-
    centrated grapefruit juice,
    thawed and undiluted
1 cup water
1 teaspoon salt
½ teaspoon pepper

2 tablespoons minced fresh parsley
½ teaspoon powdered rosemary
3 bay leaves
1 cup thinly sliced onion
3 cloves garlic, thinly sliced
2 teaspoons coarse salt
Gold Sauce

1. Boned leg of lamb will probably be a rather compact piece of meat with large pocket. With sharp knife, cut down through thinnest side of pocket and spread leg out flat, fat-side down, in large shallow baking dish.
2. Mix together olive oil, grapefruit concentrate, water, salt, pepper, parsley, rosemary and bay leaves.
3. Add onion and garlic.
4. Pour marinade over meat, cover, and marinate in refrigerator 24 hours, turning every few hours.
5. Remove from refrigerator and allow to sit at room temperature before broiling.
6. Remove from marinade, reserving marinade; sprinkle both sides with coarse salt, and place on grill set 5 to 6 inches from heat.
7. Cook 45 minutes, turning occasionally and basting with a little marinade.
8. Remove to carving board; cut against the grain into ¼-inch slices. Serve with Gold Sauce.

Gold Sauce

3 egg yolks
3 tablespoons lamb marinade
1 teaspoon cornstarch

1 teaspoon salt
⅛ teaspoon Tabasco pepper sauce
1 cup chicken broth

1 tablespoon minced parsley

1. Beat together egg yolks, lamb marinade, cornstarch, salt and Tabasco in top of double boiler; cook, stirring constantly, directly over very low heat until mixture thickens and will coat a spoon.
2. Remove mixture from heat and place over hot (not hot boiling) water in lower part of double boiler; cover and keep warm.
3. When ready to serve, stir in parsley.

Lemon-Glazed Lamb

Serves 8

5 to 6 pounds leg of lamb
¼ pound butter, melted
¼ cup lemon juice
2 tablespoons parsley, chopped
1 teaspoon dried mint leaves
1 clove garlic, peeled and minced
½ teaspoon salt

¼ teaspoon freshly ground
  black pepper
¼ cup sugar
2 cans (24 ounces) yams, drained
¼ cup butter, softened
1 egg
1 lemon slice (for garnish)

1. Remove fell (thin outer covering) from lamb.
2. Combine melted butter, lemon juice, parsley and mint leaves; add garlic that has been mashed with salt, pepper and sugar.
3. Heat, stirring constantly, until sugar melts.
4. Baste lamb well with sauce.
5. Place lamb in roasting pan on rack and roast in preheated 325° F. oven, allowing about 25 minutes per pound if fresh; 37 minutes per pound if frozen, basting frequently.
6. To decorate, mash yams and whip with butter and egg; pipe through pastry tube onto lamb.
7. Place decorated lamb in preheated 450° F. oven 5 minutes; garnish with lemon slice.

Man-of-the-House Barbecued Butterflied Leg of Lamb

Serves 6

5 to 6 pounds butterflied leg
  of lamb
1 cup wine vinegar
1 cup corn oil
½ teaspoon seasoned salt

½ teaspoon coarse ground pepper
2 teaspoons dry mustard
1 cup honey
1 large onion, sliced and
  separated into rings

1. Place butterflied leg of lamb in large bowl or crock.
2. Mix together vinegar, oil, salt, pepper, mustard and honey in 1-quart bowl; pour over meat. Add onion slices.
3. Cover and refrigerate meat mixture overnight or 12 hours, turning occasionally. Let stand at room temperature 1 hour before grilling.
4. Prepare hot bed of coals.
5. Drain lamb, reserving marinade and onion slices.
6. Grill lamb 1 to 1½ hours, depending on desired degree of doneness, brushing occasionally with marinade. (Raise grill if lamb becomes too crusted.)
7. Place onion slices in foil pouch; place on grill during last 10 to 15 minutes of cooking time. Serve as side dish.

Lamb Riblet & Fruit Skillet

Serves 4

1½ pounds lamb riblets
2 tablespoons brown sugar
1 cup fresh orange juice
1 tablespoon cornstarch

2 cups diced pineapple
1 lemon, pared and sliced
1 orange, pared and sliced
parsley (for garnish)

hot cooked rice

1. Brown lamb over low heat; cover and cook over low heat 30 minutes.
2. Drain off drippings; remove riblets.
3. Combine brown sugar, orange juice and cornstarch in skillet; blend.
4. Cook over low heat, stirring constantly, until thickened.
5. Add pineapple, lemon, orange and lamb; cover and simmer 10 minutes. Garnish with parsley; serve with rice.

Baked Lamb Shanks with Tomato Sauce

Serves 4 to 6

4 to 6 lamb shanks, about ¾ pound
  each, trimmed of fat
olive or corn oil
2 medium-size onions, cut into
  ¼-inch slices

1 teaspoon ground allspice
½ teaspoon ground nutmeg
1 teaspoon salt
½ teaspoon pepper
3 cups chopped, canned tomatoes

1. Lightly coat lamb shanks with oil; arrange in 13 x 2 x 9-inch baking dish.
2. Bake lamb in preheated 450° F. oven 30 minutes, turning once.
3. Remove lamb from oven; reduce oven temperature to 350° F.
4. Place onion slices over lamb; sprinkle with allspice, nutmeg, salt and pepper. Pour tomatoes evenly over all.
5. Return lamb to oven; bake 2 hours, or until lamb is tender, basting frequently.

Braised Lamb Shanks

Serves 4

2 tablespoons corn oil
4 lamb shanks, each weighing
  1 pound
1 onion, sliced
1 green pepper, chopped
¼ cup flour

½ teaspoon basil
½ teaspoon thyme
1 teaspoon salt
¼ teaspoon freshly ground
  black pepper
½ cup stock or bouillon

1 cup Burgundy

1. Heat oil in Dutch oven. Add lamb, onion and green pepper; cook over low heat until lamb is browned on all sides.
2. Combine flour, basil, thyme, salt and pepper; mix well and set aside.
3. Gradually add stock or bouillon, stirring constantly, until blended.
4. Add flour mixture and Burgundy to lamb; mix.
5. Cover and simmer 1½ hours, stirring occasionally, or until lamb is tender.

Mint-Glazed Lamb

Serves 5 to 6

4 to 5 pounds leg of lamb
salt
pepper
1 jar (10 ounces) mint-flavored
  apple jelly

½ cup dry white wine
2 tablespoons butter or margarine
2 tablespoons brown sugar
1 teaspoon grated lemon peel
½ teaspoon dry mustard

3 bananas, peeled and cut into large chunks

1. Sprinkle lamb with salt and pepper.
2. Roast in preheated 350° F. oven 3 hours, or until desired degree of doneness.
3. Meanwhile, combine mint jelly with wine, butter, brown sugar, lemon peel and mustard in saucepan; simmer 5 minutes.
4. Baste lamb with sauce during last hour of roasting.
5. Drop bananas in remaining mint sauce; heat for several minutes, serve as accompaniment to lamb.

Succulent Leg of Lamb with Vegetables

Serves 8

5 to 6 pounds leg of New Zealand
  spring lamb, frozen
2 cloves garlic, cut in slivers
1¾ teaspoons salt
pepper to taste
1 teaspoon dried leaf oregano

1 cup dry white wine or chicken
  broth
2 tablespoons tomato paste
4 cups water
16 small whole onions
4 large carrots, pared and cut
  in 1-inch pieces

1. Thaw lamb in refrigerator overnight.
2. Remove fell (thin outer covering) from lamb.
3. With tip of knife cut small slits in meat; insert slivers of garlic.
4. Place lamb, fat-side up, in shallow roasting pan; do not cover or add water. Insert meat thermometer into thickest part of meat, making sure tip does not rest in fat or against bone.
5. Sprinkle lamb with ¾ teaspoon salt, pepper and ½ teaspoon oregano; roast in preheated 325° F. oven 45 minutes.
6. Combine wine, tomato paste and remaining oregano in small bowl; remove lamb from oven and pour wine mixture over it.
7. Continue roasting lamb 40 minutes longer, basting after 20 minutes.
8. Bring water and remaining salt to a boil in large saucepan.
9. Cut small "X's" in stem end of each onion to prevent bursting; add onions and carrots to salted water and cook, uncovered, 10 minutes. Drain.
10. Arrange vegetables around lamb; baste lamb and vegetables with pan drippings and continue roasting 1 hour, basting every 20 minutes, until meat thermometer registers 140° F. for rare, 160° F. for medium, 170° F. or 180° F. for well done.
11. Remove lamb to serving platter; allow to "rest" 10 minutes before carving. Serve with vegetables.

Easy Lamb Kabobs

Serves 6

1½ pounds boneless shoulder of
   lamb, cut into 1-inch cubes
⅓ cup soy sauce
⅓ cup corn oil
juice of 1 lemon
½ teaspoon ground ginger

¼ teaspoon ground pepper
1 clove garlic, crushed
1 large green pepper, seeded and
   cut into 12 pieces
12 cherry tomatoes
12 green olives stuffed with
   pimiento

1. Place lamb cubes in 2-quart bowl.
2. Combine soy sauce, oil, lemon juice, ginger, pepper and garlic in measuring cup; pour over meat.
3. Cover and refrigerate several hours, or overnight.
4. Pour off marinade and set aside.
5. Assemble kabobs by alternating lamb cubes, green pepper, tomatoes and olives on skewers or bamboo sticks.
6. Grill or oven broil, turning and basting with reserved marinade until cooked on all sides to desired doneness.

Lamb Pizza Bun

Serves 8

1 lamb shoulder roast, weighing
   4 pounds
1 onion, sliced
1 teaspoon basil
½ teaspoon salt
½ teaspoon freshly ground black
   pepper
water
1 jar (15½ ounces) spaghetti sauce
1 can (6 ounces) tomato paste

1 can (4 ounces) mushrooms,
   sliced
2 teaspoons dried oregano
¼ teaspoon garlic powder
8 ounces mozzarella cheese,
   sliced
8 hamburger buns
1 green pepper, sliced in
   eight rings

1. Place lamb, onion, basil, ½ teaspoon salt and pepper in large Dutch oven; add water to cover roast.
2. Cover; bring lamb to a boil.
3. Reduce heat and simmer 3 hours, or until meat is tender.
4. Remove lamb; cool to room temperature and refrigerate.
5. Trim fat and bone from lamb; shred meat with 2 forks into strips.
6. Combine meat, spaghetti sauce, tomato paste, mushrooms, oregano and garlic powder in large skillet; mix well and simmer 15 to 20 minutes, until heated through.
7. To assemble sandwiches, place cheese slice on bottom half of each bun; spoon meat filling over cheese and top with pepper ring and bun top. Serve immediately.

Rosemary Lamb Shanks Valencia

Serves 6

6 lamb shanks
¼ cup flour
1 teaspoon salt
1 teaspoon paprika

½ teaspoon pepper
¼ cup olive oil
1 teaspoon rosemary, crushed
3 orange slices, cut in half

oven baked potatoes

1. Coat lamb shanks with mixture of flour, salt, paprika and pepper.
2. Place in shallow pan; pour oil over all and sprinkle with rosemary.
3. Bake, uncovered, in preheated 350° F. oven 2½ to 3 hours, turning occasionally, until crisp on outside.
4. If gravy is desired, mix 1 tablespoon drippings with 1 tablespoon flour. Stir in ½ teaspoon salt and 1 cup water; cook and stir over medium heat until thickened.
5. Serve meat with gravy, orange slices and oven baked potatoes.

Wine-Braised Lamb Shanks

Serves 4

1 tablespoon vegetable oil
4 New Zealand spring lamb shanks, defrosted
1½ cups thinly sliced carrots
1 small onion, chopped

1 clove garlic, minced
1 cup dry white wine
1 chicken bouillon cube
½ teaspoon salt
¼ teaspoon pepper

2 tablespoons tomato paste

1. Heat oil in large, heavy kettle; brown lamb shanks on all sides.
2. Drain off all but 2 tablespoons fat; add carrots, onion and garlic to kettle and sauté until onion is tender.
3. Add wine, bouillon, salt and pepper; bring to a boil.
4. Cover, reduce heat, and simmer 1½ hours.
5. Stir in tomato paste; simmer 30 minutes longer, or until shanks are tender.

Barbecued Lamb Shoulder

Serves 6 to 8

1 cup catsup
1 teaspoon celery salt
2 teaspoons original Worcester-shire sauce

¼ teaspoon freshly ground black pepper
¼ cup honey
5 to 6 pounds boned shoulder of lamb, rolled and tied

1. Combine catsup, celery salt, Worcestershire, pepper and honey; mix well.
2. Place lamb on spit; brush lamb with honey mixture.
3. Cook on rotisserie or outdoor grill 2 hours, or until meat thermometer registers 170° to 180° F. (depending upon desired degree of doneness), brushing lamb frequently with honey mixture during cooking.

Luscious Stuffed Lamb Shoulder

Serves 6

1 lamb shoulder, boned, weighing
   4 to 5 pounds
salt
pepper
10 slices raisin bread, diced
1 package (8 ounces) mixed dried
   fruits, diced

1 cup minced onion
1 cup minced celery and leaves
1 cup orange juice
2 teaspoons grated lemon rind
6 thick slices bacon

1. Wipe lamb shoulder inside and out with paper towels. With needle and heavy cord, sew small opening in shoulder. Sprinkle inside and out of large opening with salt and pepper.
2. Combine bread, fruits, onion and celery in large mixing bowl; pour orange juice over and sprinkle with lemon rind. Toss with fork to mix.
3. Put stuffing into lamb shoulder.
4. Set lamb roast on rack in shallow roasting pan; roast in preheated 350° F. oven 1½ hours.
5. Place bacon slices over lamb; roast 45 minutes longer.

NOTE: Any surplus stuffing can be put in greased casserole, baked, covered, for last 45 minutes, and served along with lamb.

Piquant Shoulder Lamb Chops

Serves 4 to 6

4 to 6 New Zealand spring lamb
   shoulder chops, defrosted
1 cup dry white wine
3 tablespoons wine vinegar
1 tablespoon light brown sugar
¼ teaspoon salt
1 clove garlic, minced
1 tablespoon vegetable oil

½ cup beef broth
¼ cup chili sauce
2 tablespoons finely chopped onion
1 tablespoon cornstarch
1 tablespoon water
½ cup sliced, pitted black olives
1 canned green chili, seeded
   and chopped

1. Place lamb chops in flat, shallow dish.
2. Combine wine, vinegar, brown sugar, salt and garlic; pour over chops and marinate 2 hours at room temperature, turning once.
3. Drain chops, reserving marinade; pat-dry.
4. Heat oil in large skillet; sauté chops on both sides until lightly browned.
5. Add reserved marinade, beef broth, chili sauce and onion; simmer, uncovered, 25 to 30 minutes, or until chops are tender.
6. Remove chops to serving platter; keep warm.
7. Mix cornstarch and water; add to skillet and cook, stirring, until sauce boils and thickens.
8. Add olives and green chili; spoon sauce over chops.

Teriyaki Lamb Kabobs

Serves 6

½ cup pineapple juice
¼ cup soy sauce
2 tablespoons brown sugar
¼ teaspoon ginger
⅛ teaspoon garlic salt

1½ pounds boned lamb shoulder, cut into cubes
6 slices lean bacon
6 slices canned pineapple, drained
12 California dried figs

hot cooked rice

1. Combine pineapple juice with soy sauce, brown sugar, ginger, and garlic salt.
2. Alternate lamb, bacon, pineapple and figs on skewers.
3. Place kabobs in shallow pan; pour pineapple marinade over all and refrigerate several hours.
4. Drain kabobs, reserving marinade.
5. Broil 10 minutes, brushing occasionally with sauce.
6. Turn; broil 10 minutes longer. Serve on hot rice.

Barbecued Lamb Steaks

Serves 3

⅓ cup tomato paste
⅓ cup red wine vinegar
2 tablespoons honey
¾ teaspoon dried mint, crumbled

¾ teaspoon salt
¼ teaspoon Tabasco sauce
3 lamb steaks cut from leg of New Zealand spring lamb, cut 1½ inches thick

1. Combine tomato paste, vinegar, honey, mint, salt and Tabasco in shallow dish; mix well.
2. Add lamb steaks; cover and refrigerate overnight, turning as often as possible.
3. Remove steaks; reserve marinade.
4. Arrange steaks on barbecue grill over hot coals; cook 20 minutes, until lamb is pink and juicy, turning and brushing often with marinade.

Broiled Lamb Steaks

Serves 4

2 lamb leg steaks, cut ¾ inch thick
½ teaspoon seasoned salt

½ cup stock or bouillon
1 tablespoon fresh lemon juice
2 teaspoons prepared horseradish

1. Sprinkle lamb with seasoned salt.
2. Combine stock, lemon juice and horseradish; pour over lamb.
3. Chill 1 hour, turning lamb occasionally.
4. Remove lamb from stock; reserve stock.
5. Broil lamb 3 to 4 inches from heat or cook on outdoor grill, 5 to 7 minutes.
6. Turn; cook 5 to 7 minutes, or until desired degree of doneness, brushing lamb with stock mixture frequently during cooking.

Easy Pork Parmigiana

Serves 2

1 egg
1 tablespoon water
⅓ cup seasoned bread crumbs
2 tablespoons grated Parmesan cheese

2 pork cubed steaks, 4 ounces each
2 tablespoons corn oil
1 cup Italian cooking sauce
½ cup (2 ounces) shredded mozzarella cheese

1. Beat egg and water in pie plate; combine bread crumbs and Parmesan cheese in second pie plate.
2. Dip pork steaks in crumbs, then in egg, then back in crumbs.
3. Brown pork in hot oil over moderate heat in medium-size skillet, turning once.
4. Arrange pork in 8 x 8 x 2-inch baking dish or individual casseroles; top with Italian cooking sauce.
5. Bake, uncovered, in preheated 350° F. oven until pork is done, 30 minutes, topping with mozzarella cheese during last 5 minutes.

Fiesta Pork Chops

Serves 2

2 pork loin chops, cut 1 inch thick
1 can (10 ounces) tomato pureé
⅓ cup long grain rice
¼ cup chopped onion
3 tablespoons chopped ripe olives
2 canned green chilies, seeded and chopped

1 teaspoon sugar
¼ teaspoon garlic salt
¼ teaspoon salt
¼ cup (1 ounce) shredded Monterey Jack cheese
avocado slices (for garnish)

1. Place chops in small oven roasting bag; place open bag in 8 x 8 x 2-inch baking dish.
2. Combine tomato purée in small bowl with rice, onion, olives, chilies, sugar, garlic salt and salt; pour over chops.
3. Close roasting bag with string or twist tie; bake in preheated 325° F. oven until pork is done, about 60 minutes.
4. Remove chops from roasting bag; spoon sauce over chops.
5. Top with shredded cheese; garnish with avocado slices.

Best-Yet Sizzle Pork Chops

1. Cook pork chops in skillet until tender and brown; pour off excess fat.
2. Add 2 tablespoons Worcestershire sauce; let chops sizzle in skillet a few minutes, turning to sizzle both sides.

To Microcook

1. Preheat browning skillet on HIGH 5 minutes.
2. Add 2 tablespoons Worcestershire sauce.
3. Arrange pork chops in skillet; cover with **waxed paper** and microcook on MEDIUM-HIGH 5 minutes.
4. Turn chops; continue to cook 10 to 12 minutes, rotating skillet after 4 minutes.

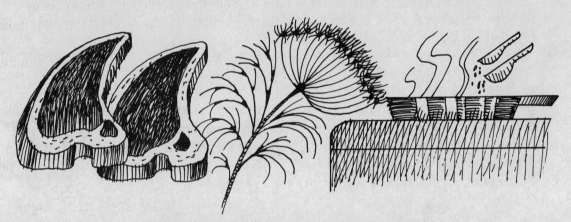

Dill-Sauced Tenderloin

Serves 2

2 pork tenderloins, 4 ounces each	1 teaspoon dried dill weed
1 egg	4 tablespoons butter or margarine
1 tablespoon water	1 tablespoon cornstarch
1 cup Swiss cheese cracker crumbs	1 cup chicken broth
1 teaspoon paprika	1 tablespoon fresh lemon juice

1. Pound tenderloins to 1/8-inch thickness; set aside.
2. Beat egg and water in pie plate; combine cracker crumbs, paprika and dill weed in second pie plate.
3. Dip tenderloins in crumbs, then in egg, then back in crumbs.
4. Melt butter in medium-size skillet; add tenderloins and cook over moderate heat until brown, about 4 minutes.
5. Turn and cook until done, about 4 minutes.
6. Remove meat from skillet and keep warm.
7. Stir cornstarch into pan drippings; add broth and cook, stirring, until thickened and bubbly.
8. Stir in lemon juice; cook 1 minute longer.
9. Spoon sauce over top of tenderloins and serve

South Pacific Pork Kabobs

Serves 2

¼ cup soy sauce
¼ cup water
¼ cup plus 2 tablespoons sliced
   green onion
3 tablespoons sugar
1 tablespoon fresh lemon juice
1 teaspoon grated fresh ginger
   root

1 clove garlic, minced
coarsely ground black pepper
¾ pound boneless pork, cut in
   1-inch cubes
3 tablespoons peanut butter
1 teaspoon cornstarch
⅓ cup milk
⅓ cup chicken broth

¼ teaspoon garlic salt

1. In small bowl, combine soy sauce, water, ¼ cup green onion, sugar, lemon juice, ginger root, garlic and ½ teaspoon pepper; add pork cubes, tossing to coat.
2. Marinate in refrigerator 8 hours, or overnight.
3. Thread pork on skewers; cook on grill over low heat until done, about 8 to 10 minutes on each side. (Or, broil at moderate temperature 3 to 5 inches from heat until done, about 8 minutes on each side.)
4. Meanwhile, blend peanut butter and cornstarch in small saucepan; stir in milk, chicken broth, 2 tablespoons green onion, garlic salt and additional dash pepper.
5. Cook sauce, stirring constantly, over moderate heat until mixture thickens and bubbles; cook 1 minute longer.
6. Serve peanut butter sauce with pork.

Hawaiian Smoked Chops

Serves 2

2 smoked pork chops, cut ½ inch
   thick
2 tablespoons corn oil
½ green pepper, thinly sliced
1 can (8¼ ounces) pineapple chunks

1 can (8 ounces) sweet potatoes,
   drained and cut in 1-inch pieces
¼ cup pineapple preserves
¼ teaspoon instant chicken
   bouillon granules

1. Brown chops in hot oil over moderate heat in skillet; remove and keep warm, reserving drippings in skillet.
2. Cook green pepper in reserved drippings over moderate heat until crisp-tender, stirring occasionally.
3. Drain pineapple chunks, reserving ¼ cup juice.
4. Add pineapple and sweet potatoes to green pepper in skillet; cook, stirring occasionally, over moderate heat until heated through.
5. Add reserved pineapple juice, pineapple preserves, bouillon granules and browned chops to skillet; cook, stirring occasionally, over moderate heat until glaze thickens, about 5 minutes.

Rathskeller Pork Dinner

Serves 2

1½ cups cooked pork, cut in
  ¾-inch cubes
½ cup water
1 teaspoon chicken bouillon
  granules

1 package (10 ounces) frozen
  Bavarian-style beans and noodles
½ teaspoon caraway seed
½ cup dairy sour cream

1. Combine pork cubes, water and chicken bouillon granules in medium-size saucepan; bring to a boil.
2. Stir in frozen bean mixture and caraway seed; cover, reduce heat, and simmer until heated through, about 3 minutes, stirring occasionally.
3. Remove from heat; stir in sour cream.

Baked Ham Slices with Tomatoes

Serves 8

8 thick slices smoked ham,
  about 4 pounds
2 cans (14½ ounces each)
  tomatoes

2 teaspoons sugar
¼ teaspoon freshly ground pepper
4 teaspoons Angostura aromatic
  bitters

½ pound sliced American cheese

1. Place ham slices in shallow baking dish.
2. Drain 1 can tomatoes; combine with other can of undrained tomatoes. Break up tomatoes into halves or smaller pieces.
3. Add sugar, pepper and Angostura aromatic bitters to tomatoes; pour mixture over ham.
4. Cover dish with lid or aluminum foil and bake in preheated 350° F. oven 20 minutes.
5. Cut cheese slices in strips; arrange over ham slices.
6. Return dish to oven for 10 to 15 minutes, or until cheese is melted and browned.

Banana Ham Patties

Serves 6

1 egg, slightly beaten
1 cup mashed ripe bananas
  (3 medium)
1 cup soft fresh bread crumbs

½ teaspoon salt
½ teaspoon prepared yellow mustard
2 cups finely chopped or ground
  cooked ham

1. Combine all ingredients and mix well; form into 6 patties.
2. Place on foil-lined baking sheet; broil for 5 minutes on each side, 3 to 5 inches from heat.
3. Serve with additional mustard.

Pork Leftover: Pork-Wild Rice Skillet

Serves 2

¼ cup chopped green onion
¼ cup chopped green pepper
2 tablespoons corn oil
1½ cups cooked pork, cut in
  ¾-inch cubes
1 package (11 ounces) frozen long-
  grain and wild rice

1 can (2½ ounces) sliced mushrooms, drained
½ cup water
2 tablespoons dry white wine
½ teaspoon instant chicken
  bouillon granules
¼ teaspoon dried basil

1 tomato, cubed

1. Cook onion and green pepper in hot oil in skillet over moderate heat until tender, stirring occasionally.
2. Stir in pork, rice, mushrooms, water, wine, bouillon granules and basil; bring to a boil.
3. Reduce heat, cover, and cook until most of the liquid is absorbed, 15 minutes, stirring occasionally.
4. Stir in tomato; cook over moderate heat until heated through, stirring occasionally.

Angostura-Stuffed Ham

Serves 10 to 12

1 smoked pre-cooked ham,
  weighing 10 to 12 pounds
¼ cup butter or margarine
1 large onion, chopped
½ cup minced celery
1 large apple, peeled, cored
  and diced
4 cups soft bread crumbs
½ cup chopped pecans or walnuts
3 teaspoons Angostura aromatic
  bitters

½ cup pineapple juice
½ cup cider vinegar
½ cup firmly packed brown sugar
mandarin orange sections (for
  garnish)
pineapple chunks (for garnish)
parsley (for garnish)
pineapple slices (for garnish)
whole spiced crab apples (for
  garnish)

1. Strip rind from ham; cut 4 slits from end to end of ham, cutting slits 1 inch apart and cutting deep to the bone.
2. Cut a small wedge out of each slit to allow room for stuffing.
3. Heat butter; sauté onion, celery and apple until tender.
4. Stir in bread crumbs, nuts, Angostura and pineapple juice.
5. Use mixture to stuff slits.
6. Place ham in a shallow roasting pan.
7. Combine vinegar and sugar; brush mixture over ham.
8. Roast ham in preheated 350° F. oven 1½ hours, basting ham with vinegar-sugar mixture every 15 minutes during cooking.
9. Garnish ham between slits with mandarin orange sections and pineapple chunks; surround with parsley and pineapple slices, topped with whole spiced crab apples.

Ham Loaf with Spicy Sauce

Serves 6

3 cups cooked ground ham
1½ cups soft bread crumbs
2 eggs, beaten slightly
1 tablespoon grated onion
⅛ teaspoon pepper
1 cup evaporated milk
2 tablespoons minced parsley
½ teaspoon dry mustard

¾ cup thinly sliced California dried figs
1 can (12 ounces) apricot juice
¼ teaspoon ground cinnamon
⅛ teaspoon nutmeg
¼ cup brown sugar
2 tablespoons fresh lemon juice
1 tablespoon cornstarch

1. Mix ham with bread crumbs, eggs, onion, pepper, milk, parsley and mustard; pack into loaf pan.
2. Bake in preheated 350° F. oven 50 minutes.
3. Meanwhile, combine figs with apricot juice, cinnamon, nutmeg, sugar, lemon juice and cornstarch; bring to a boil.
4. Simmer several minutes, stirring constantly.
5. Turn ham loaf out on platter; serve with sauce.

Spicy Crusted Ham

Allow 3 to 4 servings of ham per pound

1 boneless "fully cooked" smoked half ham
⅓ cup light brown sugar, packed
¼ cup fine dry bread crumbs
whole cloves (optional)

¼ teaspoon dry mustard
¼ teaspoon allspice
¼ teaspoon black pepper
⅓ cup light or dark corn syrup

1. Place ham, fat-side up, on rack in shallow roasting pan. Insert meat thermometer so bulb is in center of thickest part of ham; cover ham face with aluminum foil to keep it moist.
2. Bake in preheated 325° F. oven as directed on package label, or until meat thermometer registers 140° F. (It will take 2 hours for a 6 to 8-pound half ham.)
3. While ham is baking, prepare topping. Combine brown sugar, bread crumbs, mustard, allspice and pepper; mix well.
4. Bring corn syrup to a boil; set aside.
5. Thirty minutes before end of baking time, stud ham with whole cloves, if desired; brush top and sides of ham with syrup and sprinkle on about ⅓ of crumb mixture. Bake 10 minutes.
6. Drizzle with ½ of remaining syrup; sprinkle with ½ of remaining crumbs. Bake 10 minutes longer.
7. Repeat to use remaining ingredients.

Ham Steak Kaola

Serves 6

3 center-cut smoked ham slices,
1 inch thick
1 can (6 ounces) frozen pineapple-grapefruit juice concentrate

2 tablespoons hot mustard
1 tablespoon brown sugar
1 tablespoon instant minced onions

1. Place ham slices on broiler pan.
2. Combine remaining ingredients in small saucepan; cook over low heat until warmed.
3. Brush ham steaks with sauce; broil or grill with surface of ham 5 to 6 inches from heat, 15 minutes on each side, basting every 5 minutes with sauce.

Southern-Style Smothered Ham

Serves 4

2 slices ham, cut ½ inch thick,
uncooked
1 tablespoon dry mustard
2 onions, sliced

2 cups sliced pared tart apples
12 whole cloves
1 cup brown sugar
½ cup water

1. Place 1 slice ham in shallow baking pan; spread half the mustard on ham.
2. Top with onions and apples; cover with second slice of ham.
3. Rub remaining mustard onto meat; place cloves in fat portion of ham.
4. Mix sugar and water together; boil 5 minutes.
5. Pour syrup over ham; bake in preheated 350° F. oven 1 hour, basting with syrup 2 or 3 times during baking.

Flaming Strawberry Ham Glaze

Makes 12 to 15 servings

5-pound canned ready-to-eat ham
1 cup sliced strawberries

6 tablespoons orange liqueur
¼ cup light corn syrup

1. Score ham; bake according to package instructions.
2. Stir together strawberries, 2 tablespoons orange liqueur and corn syrup in small saucepan.
3. During last half hour of ham's baking time, spoon glaze over ham.
4. Remove from oven; slice.
5. Just before serving, heat remaining liqueur until vapors rise; pour over ham and ignite. Serve flaming.

NOTE: A very dramatic way to add to holiday festivities!

Peachy Ham Slices

Serves 4

2 boneless "fully cooked" ham
slices, cut ½ to ¾ inch thick
1 can (1 pound) sliced peaches,
undrained
2 tablespoons sugar

2 teaspoons cornstarch
⅛ teaspoon nutmeg
½ cup orange juice
1 tablespoon lemon juice
1 tablespoon butter or margarine

1. Cut ham slices in half; set aside.
2. Drain sliced peaches; reserve ½ cup syrup.
3. Combine and mix sugar, cornstarch and nutmeg.
4. Add peach syrup, orange juice and lemon juice; stir until free of lumps.
5. Melt butter or margarine in skillet; brown ham slices lightly on both sides.
6. Remove ham from skillet; keep warm.
7. Add cornstarch mixture to skillet; cook until thickened and clear, stirring constantly.
8. Add ham and peach slices; heat thoroughly.

Tahitian Ham & Rice

Serves 2

1 cup (5 ounces) slivered cooked ham
1 teaspoon butter or margarine
1 can (8 ounces) fruit cocktail
(drain and reserve syrup)
½ cup chicken broth or 1 chicken
bouillon cube dissolved in ½ cup
hot water
1½ tablespoons brown sugar

1 teaspoon prepared yellow
mustard
⅛ teaspoon ginger
dash of pepper
1 teaspoon soy sauce
1 tablespoon sherry (optional)
2 teaspoons cornstarch
⅓ cup diced green pepper

1 cup hot cooked rice

1. Sauté ham in butter until lightly browned.
2. Stir in fruit syrup, 2½ tablespoons broth, sugar, mustard, ginger, pepper and soy sauce; cook over low heat 5 minutes.
3. Blend remaining broth and sherry with cornstarch; stir into ham mixture.
4. Add fruit cocktail and green pepper; cook 5 minutes.
5. Serve over beds of fluffy rice.

Stuffed Glazed Ham

Serves 10

½ cup celery, chopped
2 tablespoons butter or margarine
1 cup dry bread cubes
½ cup walnuts, chopped
½ cup seedless raisins

1 cup brown sugar, packed
¼ cup prepared yellow mustard
¼ cup orange juice
1 boneless ham, about 5 pounds
whole cloves (optional)

1. Cook celery in butter in large saucepan 5 minutes; stir in bread cubes, walnuts and raisins.
2. Combine brown sugar, mustard and orange juice; add about ¼ of this to bread mixture.
3. Cut a pocket in ham with sharp knife, cutting to within about ½ inch of each edge; spoon stuffing into pocket and secure with skewers.
4. Set ham on rack in roasting pan; bake at 325° F. for about 1½ hours.
5. Remove from oven; score fat and stud with cloves, if desired.
6. Spoon brown sugar mixture over ham; increase oven temperature to 400° F. and bake 20 to 25 minutes longer until glazed.

Islander Pork Chops

Serves 4

4 pork blade steaks, cut ¾ to
　1 inch thick
3 slices bacon, cut in ¼-inch
　pieces
1 can (8¼ ounces) sliced
　pineapple

½ cup soy sauce
½ cup dry sherry
¼ cup finely chopped onion
¼ cup honey
¼ cup chili sauce
⅛ teaspoon garlic powder

1. Arrange pork steaks in shallow glass baking pan; set aside.
2. Sauté bacon in frying pan over low heat until lightly browned.
3. Drain pineapple, reserving all syrup; add pineapple syrup and remaining ingredients except pineapple slices and pork steaks to bacon; mix well.
4. Pour marinade over chops; cover and marinate 4 to 6 hours, or overnight in refrigerator, turning steaks occasionally.
5. Remove steaks, reserving marinade.
6. Place steaks on grill about 5 inches above low glowing coals; grill 14 to 16 minutes on first side; turn and grill 12 to 14 minutes longer, brushing frequently with marinade.
7. Dip pineapple slices into marinade; place on grill last 10 minutes of cooking time.
8. Serve steaks topped with pineapple slices.

Twice-Fried Pork
with Ginger Sauce

Serves 4 to 6

1 pound boneless pork
1 tablespoon soy sauce
1 tablespoon dry sherry
¼ teaspoon ground cinnamon
¼ teaspoon pepper
⅛ teaspoon ground cloves

½ cup flour
⅓ cup cornstarch
¾ cup water
about 1 quart corn oil
1 egg white
Ginger Sauce

1. Cut pork into ½-inch slices, then into 1-inch squares.
2. Stir together soy sauce, sherry, cinnamon, pepper and cloves in small bowl; add pork, tossing to coat well.
3. Cover and refrigerate while preparing batter.
4. Stir together flour and cornstarch in large bowl; gradually stir in water until smooth.
5. Stir in 1 tablespoon corn oil; let stand 30 minutes.
6. Beat egg white until stiff peaks form; fold into batter.
7. Pour oil in heavy 3-quart saucepan or deep fryer, filling no more than ⅓ full; heat over medium heat to 375° F.
8. Dip pork into batter and fry, a few pieces at a time, 3 to 4 minutes, or until pork is cooked and batter is golden; drain on paper towels.
9. Prepare Ginger Sauce. (See below.)
10. Before serving, reheat oil over medium heat to 375° F.; fry pork, a few pieces at a time, about 1 minute, or until batter is very crisp.
11. Drain on paper towels. Serve immediately with Ginger Sauce.

Ginger Sauce

Makes 2 cups

¾ cup plus 1 tablespoon water
3 tablespoons catsup
2 tablespoons soy sauce
2 tablespoons dry sherry
2 tablespoons corn oil
¼ pound snow peas
½ cup sliced water chestnuts
1 red chili pepper, diced

1 onion, cut into 8 wedges, with layers separated
1 clove garlic, minced or pressed
2 teaspoons finely grated fresh ginger or ½ teaspoon ground ginger
1 tablespoon cornstarch

1. Combine ¾ cup water, catsup, soy sauce and sherry in small bowl.
2. Heat oil in large skillet over medium heat; add snow peas, water chestnuts, pepper, onion, garlic and ginger; stir fry 2 to 3 minutes, or until vegetables are tender-crisp.
3. Add sauce mixture; bring to a boil.
4. Stir together cornstarch and 1 tablespoon water until smooth; stir into sauce mixture.
5. Bring to a boil over medium heat, stirring constantly; boil 1 minute.
6. Serve over Twice-Fried Pork.

Fruit-Glazed Butterfly Pork Chops

Serves 6

1 package (11 ounces) mixed
  dried fruit
2 tablespoons golden raisins
1½ cups white catawba grape
  juice
½ cup cream sherry

½ teaspoon dry mustard
½ teaspoon ground ginger
6 pork butterfly chops, cut 1 inch
  thick
1 tablespoon cornstarch
2 tablespoons cold water

1. Combine dried fruit, raisins, grape juice, sherry, mustard and ginger in saucepan; bring to a boil.
2. Cover and simmer until fruit is plump and tender, 25 to 30 minutes.
3. Meanwhile, place butterfly chops on rack in broiler pan; broil at moderate temperature 3 to 5 inches from heat until done, about 25 minutes, turning once.
4. Combine cornstarch and cold water in small bowl; stir into fruit mixture and cook, stirring constantly, over moderate heat until mixture is thickened and bubbly.
5. Cook 1 minute longer; spoon over chops.

NOTE: To Freeze: Place 2 cooked chops and about ¾ cup fruit mixture in moisture-vapor-proof container. Seal, label, and freeze.
To Reheat: Place frozen chops and sauce in 8 x 8 x 2-inch baking dish. Add 2 tablespoons water. Bake, covered, in preheated 400° F. oven until heated through, about 1 hour.

Plum-Jammed Pork Chops

Serves 4 to 6

6 pork chops (center cut), cut
  1 inch thick
1 tablespoon shortening
1 teaspoon seasoned salt
¼ teaspoon pepper
1 can (1 pound 4 ounces) pineapple chunks, undrained

½ cup plum jam
¼ teaspoon ground ginger
1 cup sliced celery
¼ cup sliced green onions
fluffy rice

1. Brown pork chops in shortening in 12-inch skillet.
2. Cover skillet and cook chops over low heat 1 hour, or until tender.
3. Remove chops from skillet; pour off drippings.
4. Sprinkle chops with seasoned salt and pepper.
5. Drain pineapple, reserving ½ cup syrup; add syrup and jam to skillet, blending well.
6. Stir in ginger.
7. Add pork chops; cook until mixture coats and glazes meat.
8. Stir in pineapple chunks, celery and onions, tossing until heated through.
9. Serve over fluffy rice.

Broiled Lemon Pork Chops

Serves 4

4 pork loin or rib chops, cut
  1 inch thick
⅓ cup frozen lemonade concentrate, thawed

⅓ cup currant jelly
1 tablespoon brown sugar
¼ teaspoon dry mustard
lemon slices (optional)

1. Place pork chops on rack of broiler pan.
2. Combine lemonade concentrate, currant jelly, brown sugar and dry mustard in saucepan; stir.
3. Bring to a boil; boil 2 minutes.
4. Cool slightly; brush chops with sauce.
5. Broil 4 to 5 inches from heat, 12 to 15 minutes per side; brush with sauce, turn, and brush second side with sauce.
6. If desired, place lemon slices on each chop 3 to 4 minutes before end of broiling time; brush with sauce.

Lime-Glazed Pork Chops

Serves 4

⅓ cup dark corn syrup
½ teaspoon grated lime rind
⅓ cup fresh lime juice

1 tablespoon soy sauce
¼ teaspoon ground cloves
6 pork chops, cut 1 inch thick

1. Stir together in small bowl corn syrup, lime rind, lime juice, soy sauce and cloves; set aside.
2. Grill pork chops 6 inches from heat 30 minutes, turning once.
3. Baste with lime mixture; grill 30 minutes longer, turning and basting frequently, or until pork is tender when pierced with fork and is nicely glazed.

Honolulu Pork Chops

Serves 4 to 6

6 pork chops, cut ¾ to 1 inch
  thick
1 tablespoon shortening
1 can (1 pound 4 ounces) sliced
  pineapple

½ cup teriyaki sauce
4 teaspoons cornstarch
1 tablespoon water

1. Brown pork chops slowly in shortening; pour off drippings.
2. Drain pineapple, reserving all syrup; combine syrup and teriyaki sauce.
3. Pour syrup-sauce mixture over pork chops; cover and simmer 45 minutes, or until tender.
4. Meanwhile, blend together cornstarch and water; remove chops from sauce and stir in cornstarch mixture.
5. Bring sauce to a boil; cook until sauce thickens.
6. Add chops and pineapple slices; cook only until mixture coats and glazes meat and pineapple.

Pork Chops with Milk Gravy

Serves 6

6 thick pork chops
salt to taste

pepper to taste
1½ cups cornflakes

1 to 1½ cups milk

1. Trim pork chops; reserve some pork fat in skillet with tight-fitting cover.
2. Add pork chops to fat; brown on each side. Drain off excess drippings.
3. Sprinkle chops generously with salt and pepper to taste.
4. Crush cornflakes slightly; sprinkle over chops.
5. Cover chops with milk.
6. Cover pan and bake in preheated 350° F. oven 1 hour, or until chops are tender.

Coriander Pepper Pork

Serves 4

2 cloves garlic, crushed
1 tablespoon crushed coriander
   seeds
8 crushed peppercorns
1 teaspoon brown sugar

3 tablespoons soy sauce
4 pork loin chops, cut
   1½ inches thick
grilled peach halves
grilled pineapple slices

chopped parsley (optional)

1. Combine garlic, coriander, peppercorns, brown sugar and soy sauce; brush chops well with marinade.
2. Cover; set aside 30 minutes, brushing occasionally with marinade.
3. Place chops on grill, reserving marinade.
4. Cook at moderate temperature 10 to 12 minutes per side, or until done, brushing occasionally with marinade.
5. Serve with grilled peach halves and pineapple slices dusted with chopped parsley, if desired.

Outdoor-Indoor Grilled Pork Chops

Serves 6

½ teaspoon rosemary leaves
1 tablespoon soy sauce
2 teaspoons corn oil
½ teaspoon seasoned salt

¼ teaspoon thyme leaves
¼ teaspoon sage
¼ teaspoon garlic powder
6 pork chops, cut ¾ inch thick

1. Crush rosemary; combine with remaining ingredients except pork, mixing well.
2. Brush mixture on chops.
3. Grill chops 6 inches from coals; sear on both sides.
4. Raise grill; grill slowly 35 minutes, or until well done, brushing chops occasionally with sauce.
5. To Broil Indoors: Place chops on broiler rack; broil 5 inches from heat 12 minutes per side, or until well done.

Pork Tenderloin Florentine

Serves 6

2 whole pork tenderloins,
  ¾ pound each
1 small clove garlic
1 teaspoon salt
1 package (3 ounces) cream cheese,
  at room temperature

1 package (10 ounces) frozen
  chopped spinach, thawed and
  drained
3 carrots, cut into julienne
  strips
1 chicken bouillon cube

1 cup hot water

1. Split each tenderloin lengthwise, cutting almost through to opposite side.
2. Open out flat; lay tenderloins, cut-side up, overlapping them slightly and with tips at opposite ends. Pound lightly to flatten evenly.
3. Mash garlic with salt; spread evenly over surface of meat, then spread with cream cheese.
4. Pat spinach dry; spread over cream cheese.
5. Arrange carrot strips lengthwise on spinach.
6. Roll up tenderloins, starting on wide side; tie with string at 2-inch intervals.
7. Place meat in shallow 2-quart casserole.
8. Dissolve bouillon cube in hot water; pour over meat.
9. Bake, uncovered, in preheated 325° F. oven 1 hour, or until meat is done, basting with bouillon several times.
10. Cut in ½ to ¾-inch slices to serve.

NOTE: If desired, serve tenderloin with gravy. To make: Combine ¼ cup and 1 tablespoon flour; stir until free of lumps. Add to bouillon in casserole; cook until thickened, stirring constantly. Stir in 1 teaspoon Dijon-style mustard. Serve over meat.

Pork Tenderloin with Rye Bread Stuffing

Serves 6 to 8

2 pork tenderloins
3 cups soft rye bread crumbs
2 tablespoons chopped parsley
½ teaspoon salt
⅛ teaspoon pepper
½ teaspoon caraway seeds

1 small clove garlic, minced
¼ cup chopped onion
2 tablespoons butter or margarine, melted
1 egg, slightly beaten
2 tablespoons water

1. Cut pork tenderloins lengthwise, but not quite through so they can be opened and laid flat.
2. Combine bread crumbs, parsley, salt, pepper and caraway seeds.
3. Cook garlic and onion in butter 5 minutes; add to crumb mixture.
4. Moisten stuffing with egg and water.
5. Spread stuffing on one pork tenderloin; place remaining pork tenderloin, cut-side down, on stuffing, and fasten with string or skewers.
6. Place pork on rack in an open roasting pan; roast in preheated 350° F. oven 1¼ to 1½ hours, or until done.

51

Crunchy Oriental Pork Casserole

Serves 4

1 can (10¾ ounces) condensed
   cream of mushroom soup
¼ cup milk
soy sauce
1 cup cooked pork roast, diced
1 cup celery, thinly sliced

1 can (6 ounces) water chestnuts,
   drained and sliced
1 can (3 ounces) chow mein noodles
¼ cup scallions with tops, sliced
2 tablespoons pimiento, chopped
   (optional)

1. Combine soup, milk and 1 teaspoon soy sauce; mix well.
2. Add pork, celery, water chestnuts, 1 cup noodles, scallions and pimiento; stir lightly.
3. Spoon mixture into shallow 1½-quart casserole; sprinkle with remaining noodles.
4. Bake in preheated 375° F. oven until thoroughly heated, about 20 minutes.
5. Serve with additional soy sauce, if desired.

Pork Chops with Kraut

Serves 6

6 pork rib chops, cut ½ inch thick
1 tablespoon shortening
1 cup chopped onion
1 cup coarsely chopped unpared
   raw apple

1 can (1 pound 11 ounces) sauerkraut, undrained
water
2 tablespoons light brown sugar, packed
½ teaspoon caraway seed

½ teaspoon salt

1. Brown chops in shortening on both sides in 12-inch skillet; remove chops from skillet.
2. Add onion and apple to pan drippings; heat.
3. Drain sauerkraut, reserving juice; add water to juice to make ½ cup liquid.
4. Add sauerkraut, liquid, brown sugar and caraway seed to pan.
5. Arrange chops on top; sprinkle with salt.
6. Cover and cook over low heat 30 minutes, or until chops are tender, adding additional water, a small amount at a time, if needed to keep sauerkraut moist.

Stuffed Pork Chops

Serves 6

1 package (4 ounces) stuffing
   mix for pork
1¾ cups hot water
¼ cup plus 1 tablespoon butter

1 egg, slightly beaten
6 large pork chops, cut
   1½ inches thick

1. Combine contents of seasoning packet from stuffing mix with hot water and ¼ cup butter in large mixing bowl; stir until butter is melted.
2. Stir in stuffing crumbs and egg.
3. Make a pocket in each chop by slitting from outer edge to bone; loosely stuff each pocket with stuffing and secure with wooden picks.
4. Brown chops on each side in 1 tablespoon butter in skillet; reduce heat, cover tightly, and simmer over low heat 1½ hours, or until pork is tender. (Always cook pork thoroughly.)

French-Canadian Pork Pie

Serves 6

2 pounds ground lean pork
½ cup minced onion
1 cup chopped celery
1 clove garlic, crushed
¼ cup chopped parsley
1 teaspoon salt
¼ teaspoon marjoram, crushed
⅛ teaspoon ground cloves
⅛ teaspoon ground mace

⅛ teaspoon freshly ground black
   pepper
2 cups plus 2 tablespoons
   unsifted flour
2 beef bouillon cubes
1 cup hot water
⅔ cup margarine
6 to 7 tablespoons ice water
1 egg, beaten (optional)

1. Sauté pork, onion, celery and garlic in large heavy skillet until pork is browned and vegetables are tender.
2. Stir in parsley, ½ teaspoon salt, marjoram, cloves, mace and pepper; cover and simmer 30 minutes. Drain off and discard excess fat.
3. Blend 2 tablespoons flour into skillet mixture; add bouillon cubes and hot water.
4. Return skillet to heat and bring mixture to a boil; simmer 1 minute, stirring constantly. Remove from heat; set aside.
5. Place remaining 2 cups flour and remaining salt into a bowl; cut in margarine with pastry blender or two knives until mixture resembles coarse meal.
6. Stir in ice water; mix lightly.
7. Form dough into ball, then roll out ½ dough on lightly floured board to fit a 9-inch pie plate. Transfer dough to plate; trim off extra edge, leaving ½-inch overhang.
8. Pile slightly cooked meat mixture into pie shell.
9. Roll out remaining pastry; cut 2-inch slits in center.
10. Cover pie; fold edge of top pastry under edge of lower pastry, pressing firmly together and fluting edges.
11. Brush with beaten egg, if desired.
12. Bake in preheated 400° F. oven 45 minutes, or until golden brown.

Liver Dumplings

Serves 6 to 8

½ pound pork shoulder
water to cover
1 pound pork liver, sliced
3 tablespoons lard or drippings
1 large onion, chopped
6 slices bread

2 tablespoons chopped parsley
2 eggs, beaten
½ teaspoon salt
⅛ teaspoon nutmeg
⅛ teaspoon pepper
⅓ cup stock

1. Cook pork shoulder in water until done; reserve stock.
2. Lightly brown sliced liver in lard in skillet.
3. Remove liver; brown onion in drippings. Drain.
4. Grind cooked pork with liver; combine with bread and onion. Add chopped parsley, beaten eggs, seasonings and stock. Mix well.
5. Bring stock to a boil. Drop dumplings from tablespoon into stock.
6. Cover and allow to simmer slowly 30 minutes.

Country-Style Pork Loin Ribs, Barbecued

Serves 4

3 pounds pork loin country-
style ribs
¼ cup teriyaki sauce
2 tablespoons brown sugar,
firmly packed

1 tablespoon lemon & pepper
seasoning
3 tablespoons wine vinegar
2 tablespoons corn oil
1½ teaspoons garlic powder

1 teaspoon ground ginger

1. Trim fat from ribs; cut slits halfway through meaty side between bones.
2. Combine remaining ingredients; mix well.
3. Grill ribs 6 inches from coals, cooking 45 minutes, or until well done; turn and brush frequently with sauce.
4. To broil indoors, place ribs on broiler rack 5 inches from heat; broil 40 minutes, or until well done, turning and brushing often.

Mustard-Glazed Ribs

Serves 4

4 pounds country-style ribs,
trimmed and cut in serving pieces
water

½ cup dark corn syrup
½ cup prepared spicy brown mustard
¼ cup cider vinegar

1. Place spareribs with water to cover in 5-quart saucepot; cover and bring to a boil over high heat.
2. Reduce heat and boil gently 1 hour, or until tender.
3. Stir together remaining ingredients in small bowl.
4. Drain ribs well; brush generously with sauce.
5. Grill ribs 5 inches from heat, turning and basting frequently, about 15 minutes, or until browned.

Pork Liver Cantonese

Serves 4

4 slices bacon
⅓ cup chopped onion
⅓ cup pineapple chunks
¼ cup chopped green pepper
½ cup packed brown sugar
3 tablespoons pineapple juice

2 tablespoons cider vinegar
1 teaspoon soy sauce
⅛ teaspoon dried basil
⅛ teaspoon dried thyme
1 pound pork liver, cut
  ½ inch thick

pepper to taste

1. Cook bacon in medium-size skillet over moderate heat until crisp.
2. Remove bacon, reserving drippings in skillet.
3. Crumble bacon and set aside.
4. Add onion, pineapple and green pepper to reserved drippings; cook, stirring occasionally, over moderate heat until vegetables are tender.
5. Stir in brown sugar, pineapple juice, vinegar, soy sauce, basil, thyme, and reserved bacon; season to taste with pepper.
6. Place liver in 12 x 7½ x 2-inch baking dish; pour sauce over liver.
7. Bake in preheated 350° F. oven until liver is done, about 25 minutes.

Smokey Pork Ribs

Serves 4 to 6

4 to 6 pounds pork country-style
  ribs, cut 1 inch thick
water
3 cloves garlic, chopped
2 tablespoons butter
1 teaspoon original Worcestershire sauce

1 tablespoon hickory liquid smoke
2 tablespoons brown sugar
1 cup catsup
½ teaspoon salt
1 teaspoon pepper

1. Place ribs in large saucepan; cover with water and bring to a boil.
2. Reduce heat, cover, and simmer for 20 minutes.
3. Meanwhile, brown garlic in butter in saucepan 2 to 3 minutes; add ¼ cup water and remaining ingredients and bring to a boil.
4. Reduce heat, cover, and simmer 10 minutes, stirring occasionally.
5. Place ribs on grill; cook 20 minutes, turning and brushing with sauce every 5 minutes.

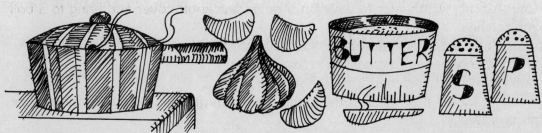

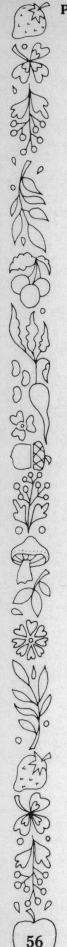

Fruited-Stuffed Spareribs

Serves 8

2 racks pork spareribs, weighing
   about 6 pounds
1 teaspoon seasoned salt
⅛ teaspoon pepper
1 can (1 pound 4 ounces) crushed
   pineapple, drained

2 cups cooked rice
¾ cup toasted coconut
½ cup sliced almonds
3 tablespoons teriyaki sauce
1 egg, beaten

1. Sprinkle spareribs with seasoned salt and pepper.
2. Place one rack in large roasting pan.
3. Mix together all remaining ingredients; spread over spareribs.
4. Top with second rack of ribs; cover tightly with foil.
5. Roast in preheated 450° F. oven 1 hour.
6. Uncover pan, reduce heat to 325° F., and continue roasting 1 to 1½ hours longer.

Crown Roast of Pork with Rice d'Orange

Serves 7 to 8 (2 ribs each)

1 crown roast of pork, 14 to
   16 ribs
red pepper
1 cup chopped onions
1 tablespoon butter or margarine
1 teaspoon thyme
½ cup seedless raisins

½ cup orange juice
¼ cup dry sherry
6 cups hot cooked rice, cooked
   in chicken broth
2 tablespoons grated orange peel
2 oranges, peeled and sectioned
   (for garnish)

1. Season inside and out of crown roast with ½ teaspoon salt and red pepper.
2. Place roast, ribs down, in shallow pan; roast in preheated 325° F. oven, basting occasionally, 2½ hours, or until meat at center registers 175° F. on meat thermometer.
3. Meanwhile, sauté onions in butter until soft but not brown.
4. Add remaining salt, thyme, raisins, orange juice and sherry; cover and cook over low heat 5 minutes, or until raisins are plump.
5. Stir in cooked rice and 1 teaspoon orange peel, tossing lightly to blend well.
6. Fifteen minutes before meat is done, remove from oven and pour off pan juices, reserving, if desired, to make gravy.
7. Turn roast, ribs up; fill center with orange rice and spoon remaining rice around roast.
8. Cover with foil to prevent drying of rice and return to oven until meat is fully cooked.
9. Sprinkle with remaining orange peel and garnish with orange sections before serving.

NOTE: Festive and tasty!

Spicy Barbecued Ribs

Serves 4

1 cup catsup
2 tablespoons original Worcestershire sauce
¼ cup prepared yellow mustard
1½ tablespoons cider vinegar

1 tablespoon prepared horseradish
1 teaspoon sugar
¾ teaspoon garlic powder
½ teaspoon salt
⅛ teaspoon ground black pepper

3 to 4 pounds pork spareribs

1. Combine catsup, Worcestershire, mustard, vinegar, horseradish, sugar, garlic powder, salt and pepper; set aside.
2. Place ribs on rack in shallow roasting pan; bake, uncovered, in preheated 450° F. oven 15 minutes.
3. Turn over and bake 15 minutes longer.
4. Remove from oven; drain off drippings.
5. Reduce oven to 325° F.; spoon half the barbecue sauce over ribs and bake, uncovered, for 20 minutes.
6. Turn ribs and brush with remaining sauce; bake until well glazed and done, about 20 minutes. (To test for doneness, make a cut near the center of a meaty portion and be sure no pink remains.)
7. Or, place partially cooked ribs on a grill 4 inches from hot coals; brush on half of reserved sauce and barbecue 10 minutes. Turn over, brush on remaining barbecue sauce, and barbecue 10 minutes longer.

NOTE: Delicious!

Herb-Seasoned Pork Steaks

Serves 4

1 egg
3 tablespoons milk
1 cup herb-seasoned stuffing mix,
crushed

¼ cup grated Parmesan cheese
4 pork cubed steaks
2 to 4 tablespoons shortening

1. In pie plate, beat egg and milk with a fork until combined.
2. Combine stuffing mix and Parmesan cheese in another pie plate; mix well.
3. Dip steaks in crumbs, then in egg mixture, then in crumb mixture again.
4. Cook in hot shortening over medium heat 5 to 7 minutes; turn and continue cooking 5 to 7 minutes, or until browned and steaks are done.

Ginger-Glazed Loin Pork Roast

Serves 6

1 tablespoon cornstarch	3 tablespoons Worcestershire sauce
½ cup firmly-packed brown sugar	½ teaspoon ginger
¼ cup vinegar	¼ teaspoon salt
	4 pounds pork loin roast

1. Stir together cornstarch and brown sugar in small saucepan; add vinegar, Worcestershire, ginger and salt.
2. Cook, stirring occasionally, until mixture comes to a boil and thickens slightly.
3. Brush some of the glaze over pork; roast, uncovered, in preheated 325° F. oven 35 minutes per pound, or until meat thermometer reads 170° F., brushing with remaining glaze several times during roasting.

MICROWAVE DIRECTIONS: Stir together glaze ingredients in small bowl. Microcook on HIGH 2 minutes, stirring once or twice. Brush roast with glaze. Cover with plastic wrap. Microcook on MEDIUM 13 to 15 minutes per pound, rotating dish several times. Brush with remaining glaze, and microcook on MEDIUM 3 to 5 minutes, or until thoroughly cooked.

Herbed Pork Roast with Peppers

Serves 6 to 8

1 clove garlic	½ teaspoon oregano
1 teaspoon salt	¼ teaspoon leaf thyme
4 to 5 pounds pork loin roast, with bone loosened	1 cup sliced onion
	2 green peppers, cut in strips
½ teaspoon crushed rosemary	2 sweet red peppers, cut in strips

1. Mash garlic with ½ teaspoon salt; rub over surface of roast.
2. Combine herbs; rub over roast.
3. Place roast, fat-side up, on rack in shallow roasting pan; insert meat thermometer so bulb is in center of thickest part of roast, not touching bone.
4. Roast, uncovered, in preheated 325° F. oven 2 to 2½ hours, or until meat thermometer registers 170° F.
5. Place roast on warm serving platter; keep warm.
6. Drain fat off pan drippings; add onion to pan drippings and cook 5 minutes.
7. Add peppers, sprinkle with remaining salt, and cook until peppers are tender, stirring occasionally. Serve around roast.

NOTE: Have butcher loosen chine (back) bone by sawing across rib bones.

Savory-Sauced Rice with Roast Loin of Pork

Serves 6

1 cup chopped onions
2 tablespoons butter or margarine
3 cups cooked rice
3 tablespoons chopped pimientos
1 teaspoon salt
dash ground black pepper
⅓ cup dairy sour cream

3 tablespoons real mayonnaise
1 teaspoon lemon juice
¼ teaspoon curry powder
hot cooked rice
¼ cup crumbled crisp bacon
   (optional)
5 to 6 pounds cooked roast loin of pork

1. Cook onions in butter in large skillet until tender.
2. Stir in rice; heat thoroughly.
3. Add pimientos, salt and pepper; toss lightly.
4. Combine sour cream, mayonnaise, lemon juice and curry powder; spoon over beds of rice; top with bacon.
5. Serve with sliced roast loin pork for each person.

Orange-Glazed Pork Roast

Serves 8 to 10

4 to 5 pounds boneless pork loin
   roast (double loin, rolled and tied)
1½ teaspoons ginger
¼ cup frozen orange juice concentrate, thawed

¼ cup honey
orange slices (optional garnish)
lime slices (optional garnish)
fresh pineapple spears
   (optional garnish)

watercress (optional garnish)

1. Rub roast surface with 1 teaspoon ginger.
2. Place roast on rack in shallow roasting pan; insert meat thermometer so bulb is in center of thickest part of roast.
3. Roast, uncovered, in preheated 325° F. oven 2½ hours, or until meat thermometer registers 170° F.
4. Meanwhile, combine orange juice concentrate, honey and remaining ginger; bring to a boil.
5. Boil 1 minute; cook slightly.
6. Brush sauce over roast several times during last 30 minutes of cooking time; let stand 15 minutes before slicing.
7. Garnish with orange and lime slices, pineapple spears and watercress, if desired.

Pork Pot Roast à la William Tell

Serves 6

4 pounds boneless pork Boston
  shoulder roast
1 teaspoon dried thyme
2 cups apple juice or cider
1 tablespoon cider vinegar
3 medium potatoes, pared and
  quartered

3 medium carrots, cut in ½-inch
  pieces
2 stalks celery, cut in 1-inch
  pieces
1 large onion, cut in wedges
1 medium apple, pared and cut
  in wedges

salt to taste
pepper to taste

1. Sprinkle roast with thyme; place in 4-quart Dutch oven.
2. Add apple juice and vinegar to roast; bring to a boil.
3. Cover, reduce heat, and simmer 1½ hours.
4. Add potatoes, carrots, celery, and onion to roast; return to a boil.
5. Cover; reduce heat, and simmer until pork and vegetables are tender, about 1 hour.
6. Add apple wedges to roast during last 15 minutes of cooking time.
7. Season to taste with salt and pepper.
8. Skim off fat from pan juices; pass pan juices with roast and vegetables.

Pork Sausage Pie

Serves 6

1 pound pork sausage
1 cup chopped onion
1 cup chopped celery
1 cup diced potato, pared

2 tablespoons flour
¼ teaspoon salt
¼ teaspoon mace
1 cup water

pastry for 9-inch double-crust pie

1. Cook sausage until lightly browned; drain off excess fat.
2. Add onion, celery and potato; stir and heat thoroughly.
3. Stir in flour, salt and mace; add water and cook until thickened, stirring constantly.
4. Cover and simmer 15 minutes; uncover and simmer to thicken, if needed. Cool.
5. Divide pastry in half. On lightly floured board roll out half the pastry into a circle about ⅛-inch thick. Fit crust into 9-inch pie plate; trim crust.
6. Roll out remaining pastry; cut small slits for vents.
7. Fill lined pie plate with sausage mixture.
8. Moisten edge of crust; cover with top crust and press edges together.
9. Trim crust; seal and flute edges.
10. Bake in preheated 400° F. oven until crust is brown and filling is bubbling, 30 to 35 minutes.
11. Let stand 10 to 15 minutes before serving. Cut into wedges.

Blanquette de Veau

Serves 4 to 6

1 can (10¾ ounces) condensed
  chicken broth
2 pounds boneless veal, cut
  into 1½-inch cubes
2 tablespoons chopped parsley
1 small clove garlic, minced
1 teaspoon lemon juice
½ teaspoon thyme, crushed

generous dash ground cloves
1 pound (about 16) small whole
  white onions
2 cups small fresh mushroom
  caps, (about ½ pound)
¾ cup light cream
3 tablespoons flour
hot cooked rice

1. Combine broth, veal, parsley, garlic, lemon juice, thyme and cloves in skillet; cover and cook over low heat 1 hour.
2. Add onions and mushrooms; cook 30 minutes longer, or until meat and vegetables are tender.
3. Gradually blend cream into flour until smooth; slowly stir into sauce and cook, stirring, until thickened.
4. Serve over hot cooked rice.

Curried Barbecued Veal Chops

Serves 4

¼ cup corn oil
1 small onion, minced (⅓ cup)
1 clove garlic, minced, or
  ¼ teaspoon garlic powder
2 to 3 tablespoons curry powder

¼ cup vinegar
¼ cup dark or light corn syrup
scant teaspoon salt
¼ teaspoon pepper
4 chops (veal, pork or lamb)

1. Heat corn oil in small skillet over medium-low heat; add onion, garlic and curry powder.
2. Cook 2 minutes, stirring occasionally, or until tender.
3. Remove from heat; stir in vinegar, corn syrup, salt and pepper until well mixed.
4. Place chops in shallow baking dish; pour curry mixture over chops.
5. Cover and refrigerate overnight, turning occasionally.
6. Remove chops from marinade; grill 4 inches from heat, brushing with curry mixture and turning as needed, 10 to 15 minutes, or until desired doneness.

Veal Delight

Serves 6

2 veal round steaks, cut ½ inch thick
2 tablespoons lard or drippings
1 can (4 ounces) sliced mushrooms, undrained
1 green pepper, cut into 1-inch squares

2 tablespoons butter or margarine
3 tablespoons flour
2 cups milk
1 package (1½ ounces) dehydrated onion soup
¼ cup 1-inch squares pimientoes

1. Cut steaks into 6 servings; pound to ¼-inch thickness.
2. Brown steaks in lard; pour off drippings.
3. Drain mushrooms, reserving liquid; cook mushrooms in butter until tender.
4. Stir in flour, milk, reserved mushroom liquid and onion soup; cook, stirring constantly, until thickened.
5. Place veal steaks in greased 8 x 12-inch baking dish; pour sauce over steaks and place pimientoes on top.
6. Cover and bake in preheated 300° F. oven 30 minutes; uncover and continue baking 15 minutes, or until tender.

Veal Paprikash

Serves 6

2 tablespoons instant minced onion
water
2 pounds boneless veal shoulder
5 tablespoons flour
1 teaspoon salt

¼ teaspoon ground black pepper
¼ cup salad oil
2 tablespoons paprika
1 tablespoon butter or margarine
½ cup milk
1 cup dairy sour cream

cooked broad noodles (optional)

1. Rehydrate minced onion in 2 tablespoons water 10 minutes.
2. Cut veal into 1-inch cubes; dredge meat with 4 tablespoons flour mixed with salt and black pepper.
3. Heat oil in skillet; add meat, onion and 1 tablespoon paprika. Brown meat well on all sides.
4. Add ⅓ cup water; cover tightly and simmer 45 minutes, or until meat is tender, turning occasionally. (Add more water if needed.)
5. Melt butter in small saucepan; blend in remaining flour and paprika; cook and stir until mixture bubbles.
6. Remove from heat; gradually stir in milk.
7. Return to heat; bring rapidly to a boil, stirring constantly.
8. Reduce heat and cook, stirring 1 to 2 minutes longer, or until thickened.
9. Gradually blend in sour cream, beating vigorously.
10. Pour sauce over cooked meat in skillet; heat thoroughly, but do not boil.
11. Serve hot with broad noodles, if desired.

Lettuce Scaloppine

Serves 4

1 head western iceberg lettuce
4 servings veal, cut for
   scaloppine
salt
pepper
1 egg, lightly beaten

½ cup cheese cracker crumbs
¼ cup shortening
1 can (8 ounces) tomato sauce
1 tablespoon butter or margarine
1 teaspoon vinegar
½ teaspoon Worcestershire sauce

1. Core, rinse, and thoroughly drain lettuce; chill in lettuce crisper or plastic bag.
2. Pound veal lightly, sprinkle with salt and pepper, dip in egg, and roll in crumbs.
3. Heat shortening in skillet; add veal and sauté slowly 5 to 7 minutes on each side, or until lightly browned.
4. Meanwhile, combine tomato sauce, butter, vinegar and Worcestershire in saucepan; heat, stirring occasionally.
5. Cut lettuce crosswise across heart with sharp knife to make 4 thin rafts. (Chill remaining lettuce in plastic bag or plastic wrap for use another time.)
6. Arrange leaf rafts on dinner plates or serving platter; sprinkle lightly with salt.
7. Place veal on lettuce; spoon sauce over veal and serve at once.

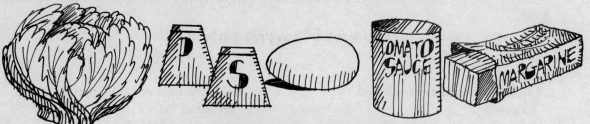

Veal Chops with Squash

Serves 6

3 tablespoons flour
½ teaspoon salt
½ teaspoon garlic salt
½ teaspoon basil leaves
¼ teaspoon rosemary leaves,
   crushed
⅛ teaspoon pepper

6 veal rib chops, cut ¾ inch
   thick
2 tablespoons cooking oil
water
1 can (10 ounces) tomatoes,
   undrained
3 zucchini, cut into ½-inch
   slices

1. Combine flour, salt, garlic salt, basil, rosemary and pepper; dredge chops in flour mixture, reserving excess seasoned flour.
2. Brown meat in oil in large skillet; pour off drippings.
3. Add ½ cup water, cover tightly, and cook slowly 45 minutes.
4. Drain tomatoes, reserving liquid.
5. Add enough water to tomato liquid to make 1 cup.
6. Combine reserved seasoned flour with tomato liquid and stir into cooking liquid; bring to a boil, stirring constantly.
7. Add tomatoes, broken up, and zucchini; continue cooking, covered, 15 minutes.

Veal Scallops, Viennese Style

Serves 4 to 6

4 thinly sliced veal scallops
(about 1 pound)
½ teaspoon salt
½ teaspoon ground black pepper
2 tablespoons flour
½ cup milk

1 egg, beaten
½ cup finely ground dry bread
crumbs
½ cup sweet butter, softened
2 tablespoons fresh lemon juice
1 to 2 tablespoons anchovy paste

½ cup clarified sweet butter

1. Season veal with salt and pepper.
2. Coat veal on both sides with flour; shake off excess flour and let stand about 10 minutes.
3. Combine milk and egg; dip veal in milk mixture, then coat on both sides with bread crumbs. Let stand 10 minutes.
4. Meanwhile, beat softened butter, lemon juice and anchovy paste until well blended and smooth; put in pastry tube fitted with star tip and set aside.
5. Heat clarified-butter in heavy sauté or fry pan over medium heat just until it begins to smoke slightly; add veal and cook until lightly browned, 45 to 50 seconds on each side.
6. To serve; pipe about 1 tablespoon anchovy butter into a rosette on top of each scallop.

Wiener Schnitzel

Serves 4

1½ pounds veal cutlets
seasoned flour
1 slightly beaten egg
2 to 3 teaspoons water or milk

2 teaspoons corn oil
¾ cup sifted seasoned dry bread
crumbs
½ to ¾ cup butter

lemon slices (for garnish)

1. Pound cutlets to ¼-inch thickness; wipe dry with clean cloth.
2. Combine egg, water and oil in bowl.
3. Flour cutlets, shaking or patting to remove excess flour; slide flour-coated cutlets through egg mixture, allowing excess moisture to drain off.
4. Place cutlets in bowl lined with bread crumbs; press so that crumbs adhere evenly to all edges and surfaces of cutlets.
5. Place on a wire rack to dry for 20 minutes.
6. Melt butter in large skillet; sauté chops over low heat 2 minutes on one side; turn and cook 2 minutes on other side.
7. Turn again and cook until done, not more than another 5 to 6 minutes.
8. Remove to heated platter; garnish with lemon slices.